You Everywhere Now: Get Your Message, Products and Services In Front of Your Target Prospects and in Every Pocket, Screen, Car and Television In the World with the Help of the Largest Brands in the World, FREE!

Mike Koenigs

You Everywhere Now: Get Your Message, Products and Services In Front of Your Target Prospects and in Every Pocket, Screen, Car and Television In the World with the Help of the Largest Brands in the World, FREE!

Register This Book and Get Free Updates and Free Videos

To get updates to this book and access to four interactive videos that will show you how to grow your business with the strategies in this book and an invitation to two interactive online livecasts to meet the author and his team, visit www.TrafficGeyser.com/BookBonus or text YEN to 58885 or text your email address to (858) 866-8812 or scan this QR Code:

Table Of Contents

Register This Book   3

About The Author   5

About This Book   9

Special Thanks To   14

READ ME FIRST: How to Get the Most Out   20
of This Book

Intro: How to Get the Biggest Brands in the   25
World to Give You Their Customers for Free

Marketing Lessons from Buddha, Jesus   32
Christ, Krishna, Mohammed, and Gandhi:
How to Instantly Get Your Message on the
Screens and in the Pockets of All of Your
Target Prospects

The Power of Multicasting: Create Once,   38

Distribute Everywhere

How to get Raving Fans and Loyal Customers like Apple does — 42

How to Easily Partner with Big Brands and Seduce their Customers — 47

How to Become a Celebrity in Your Market so that You can Persuade and Influence Sales — 51

How to Get Expert Status in the Shortest Time Possible so that You can Dominate Your Market — 54

How to Build Your Online Power and Influence as Fast as Possible so that You Can Stand Out and Dominate Your Niche or Industry — 57

How to Make a Perfect Video Testimonial — 60

How to Capture a Perfect Testimonial with an Interview — 65

What's Next? — 68

About Traffic Geyser — 73

About Instant Customer — 78

About The Author

Four-time #1 Bestselling Author, "2009 Marketer of the Year" winner, serial entrepreneur, filmmaker, speaker and patented inventor, **Mike Koenigs** is the CEO, "Chief Disruptasaurus" and Founder of Traffic Geyser, Instant Customer and creator of "Author Expert Marketing Machines", "Make, Market Launch IT" and "The Top Gun Consulting Toolkit". His products and services have simplified and automated marketing for over 30,000 small businesses, authors, experts, speakers, coaches and consultants in over 60 countries.

Mike is a recent (2013) stage 3a cancer survivor, completing major surgery, 4 months of chemotherapy, 33 radiation treatments and has recovered thanks to integrative, nutritional, alternative, energy therapies and meditation. He is very grateful to be alive.

His vision and goal is to create 1,000,000 entrepreneurs in his lifetime in both the developed and developing world. An active philanthropist, Mike has raised nearly $2mm for the "Just Like My Child" foundation, www.JustLikeMyChild.org, a non-profit 501c3 organization that provides education, microfinance, entrepreneurship, girls education and legal rights in Uganda and Senegal.

Mike's companies have produced ten consecutive online product launches with the largest grossing over $9.1 million dollars in one week. In a single "direct to camera" webcast, Mike produced over $3.1 million dollars in sales in one day. His celebrity and bestselling author clients and friends include Paula Abdul, Tony Robbins, Richard Dreyfuss, Peter Diamandis, John Assaraf, Brian Tracy, Jorge Cruise, and Harvey MacKay.

He produced the award-winning feature film "Bill's Gun Shop", distributed by Warner Brothers and the feature documentary, "Life With Tesla" about going all-solar and gasoline-free with an electric car. He's appeared in Inc., Success Magazine, Fortune and on ABC, NBC and Fox Networks.

Originally from Minnesota, Mike lives in San Diego, CA with his wife and son. He loves the ocean, is an avid boater, and plays the "didgeridoo."

Mike can be reached at his personal web site at www.MikeKoenigs.com

Facebook: www.FaceBook.com/koenigs

Twitter: @MikeKoenigs

Other Books By Mike Koenigs:

- Author Expert Marketing Machines: The Ultimate 5-Step, Push-Button, Automated System to Become the Expert, Authority and Star in Your Niche

- Make Market Launch IT: The Ultimate Product Creation System for Turning Your Ideas Into Income

- Podcast Strategies: How To Podcast - 21 Questions Answered

- Multicast Marketing: How to Podcast, Publish and Promote Your Content to the World with Google Hangouts, YouTube Live, Kindle Books, Mobile and Social Media

About This Book

Every once in a while a revolutionary new product comes along that completely transforms the marketplace...

In 1876, the telephone was invented, changing communications forever and allowing anyone with a phone to communicate quickly and efficiently, replacing telegraph and telegrams.

A little more than 100 years later, the world wide web reshaped the way we think and do business, making communications and content distribution free and allowing you to buy, sell or market anything, anywhere,

6

anytime, from any device. The internet and mobile devices have been replacing newspapers, radio, television, even books.

Apple, Google/YouTube, Amazon and Facebook built and control multibillion dollar distribution networks on the Internet...and together, they and a few dozen other social networking companies "own" the screens, eyes and ears of 73% of the human race that are engaged on those networks...clicking ads, buying products and services, consuming content...

My guess is you're here right now because you have a mission, a purpose, a product, a desire for a lifestyle change, control over what you do and how you do it... You're here because you want more money, get paid for who you are, not what you do, are overwhelmed with the latest tools, software, social media, tech stuff and maybe you're just just getting started...

I know what that feels like. It's why my passion has been to help people get unstuck from tech and marketing quicksand and and get seen, heard and noticed, to have impact and make a difference. If this sounds like you, then you're in the right place at the right time!

What if there was a way to have everything you need in one system so you can broadcast your message to the connected planet while simultaneously having this same system doing all of your marketing, lead capture, follow up and sales?

And what if it worked and connected with all of the systems you already have in place? And what if there were people standing by to help you build your first marketing campaigns with you?

This book will introduce you to a complete, proven, integrated system that combines tools and training to get **YOU EVERYWHERE NOW**, on every screen, in every pocket, desktop, laptop, smartphone, tablet, car, television. Literally in front of billions of people. So they can find and learn about you, your products and services anytime, anywhere, on any device.

By the time you finish reading this book and reviewing the videos available in a free series, you'll understand how to reach and connect with 73% of human race - who are engaged with social, video and mobile networks right now.

```
To get free updates to this book and an interactive video
version of this book that will show you how to share your
message, products and services with the connected planet,
visit www.TrafficGeyser.com/BookBonus or text YEN to 58885
      or text your email address to (858) 866-8812
```

Mike KoenigsSan Diego, California
You Everywhere Now
April 2014

Special Thanks To

Vivian Glyck and Zakary Koenigs, my incredibly patient wife, son and my family, Mom, Dad, Ellen, Rick, Joel. I love you all so much. You are reminders the amazing gift life is.

Chris and Pam Hendrickson, best of friends and my family here in San Diego

Arielle Ford and Brian Hilliard, your unconditional love and support keeps me connected to the divine when I lose my way.

Debbie Ford. RIP. I miss you, your spirit, sarcasm, cancer guidance, friendship and commitment to truth. Thank you for showing me my shadow when I didn't want to see it.

Gene Naftulyev my friend who helped restore my business health when my health failed.

Ed Rush who became my marketing savior and voice when I didn't have one...I'd take a bullet for you, brother.

Paul Colligan for his genius, creative mind and kind

heart. I love making things with you.

Laurie Hull, my PA for your tireless, willingness to put up with my drama and BS for years.

Jessie Schwartzburg, you're an entrepreneur's dream and you make us (and me) look good with every event you touch.

My incredible team at Instant Customer and Traffic Geyser past and present: Helen, Oliver, Rick, Robin, Anthony, Melyssa, Sean, Felissa, Camilla. I've never worked with a more committed, dedicated group of people who really care and do the right thing for our customers and clients.

My mastermind brothers: Ed Rush, John Assaraf, Darren Hardy, Eric Berman, Greg Habstritt, Bob Serling, Steven Cox, Matt Trainer. You guys are an inspiration and motivating force that helped keep me alive when I almost died last year.

Suresh and Liz for helping with this copy and editing.

My wonderful customers and clients. You're my inspiration and mission! It's an honor and a privilege to serve and support you.

Joe Polish - thank you for your kindness and support over the past ten years.

And everyone else I may have forgotten to give thanks and praise to.

READ ME FIRST:
How to Get the Most
Out of This Book

---

*"Once you make a decision,
the universe conspires to make it happen."*

Ralph Waldo Emerson

Good. You've taken the first step. You have this book and you're reading it.

Even if you've read other books, this one is different because until just a few weeks ago, much of what is discussed in this book wasn't possible until now.

If you use what's here, it will forever change the way you think about marketing, content and building a business. Any business.

I know you're super busy, overwhelmed and looking for some ways to get ahead.

My guess is you want a lifestyle change, more control

over what you do and how you do it... You want to get paid more for who you are, not what you do and are probably overwhelmed with all the tricky tools and tech, software, social media...maybe you're just getting started...

The first thing you should do is sign up for the free videos - details are below.

When you register for the free videos, you'll also get notified when this book is updated - it's a work in progress and will change based on the feedback and comments I receive.

Next, attend one of our "livecasts" - a high-quality, interactive online event. When you register for the free videos, you'll be registered automatically and an invitation link to join us. There, you'll meet me and my team and have a chance to experience everything we talk about in this book first-hand with live-chat and interactivity. They're fun and you'll learn a ton.

Next, skim through this book and read whatever jumps out and speaks to you. I'm a big believer in trusting intuition. Trust your gut.

The #1 lesson to walk away with is from this book is great marketing is 90% psychology and 10% technology. There are lots of personal stories I share in this book and all of them a relevant to practically business.

Next, I'll share some transformational stories that will help you learn more, faster. I hope you'll be inspired by them and use the lessons to get more results and impact in your life.

Everything in this book works - in fact, I wrote this book using the system from start to finish **in less than a month**. It's my fifth book in less than 18 months - and this same model has been used successfully by thousands of other customers all over the world. It can work for you too.

Here's a warning. Don't delay. Take imperfect action. The Internet and the web is growing at an amazing pace. The world will continue to get more competitive, people will feel even more overwhelmed and get busier. Right now, it's easier and more affordable than ever before to be seen, heard and found.

But that might change a day, a week, a month or a year from now and the sooner you get started and learn the the incredible skills found in "You Everywhere Now", you can accomplish your dreams by sharing your message, products, services and you with the world.

To get free updates to this book, an interactive video version of this book that will show you how to share your message, products and services with the connected planet and an invitation to attend a free interactive livecast, **visit www.TrafficGeyser.com/BookBonus or text YEN to 58885 or text your email address to (858) 866-8812**

Intro: How to Get the Biggest Brands in the World to Give You Their Customers for Free

> *"Business has only two functions - marketing and innovation."*
>
> Milan Kundera

I believe we live in the greatest moment in human history.

With the click of a button, you can communicate and interact with more than 80% of the connected planet.

Mobile and online technology are disrupting virtually every business and government in the world. At the same time, these technologies are raising the standard and quality of life for almost every person on the planet by providing education and accountability for nearly everyone.

More than ever before, entrepreneurs are starting their own businesses, and there are more resources available than at any other time in the history of the world.

With simple, affordable technology, you, your message, your products, and services can be seen, heard, shared, and put in the pockets of your target prospects.

Your message can be viewed or listened to on billions of smartphone screens, computers, tablets, televisions and even in the cars of every person, prospect, or business in the world with the click of a button — and all of this can be done FOR FREE.

If you know the right formula to create engaging content, the biggest brands in the world including Google, Apple, Amazon, Facebook, YouTube, Twitter, LinkedIn, and hundreds more will actively promote, market, and share you with the world for free - and some will promote and pay you for that privilege.

We know it's a big idea, and that's why we call it *"You. Everywhere. Now."*

Here's a basic "pitch" video script we wrote for a YouTube video advertising we're that describes the *"You. Everywhere. Now."* vision:

```
What if, with the click of a button,
your message could reach billions of
people and be seen on any device,
```

anywhere, anytime?

This is YouTube - seeing is believing - click this button and I'll show one simple system that can make it happen for you.

In the past, this has been a nightmare to make this work - complicated, time-wasting and really expensive. Click this button right now to see how easy it is to get your message out to the world - without the hassle...

There's a really cool tool that will let you upload your message once and with the click of a button, instantly distribute it to the best video, social media and networking sites including Google, Apple, YouTube, Amazon, Facebook, Twitter, LinkedIn and many more to billions of smartphones, tablets, laptop and desktop computers...even cars and televisions. There's no limit to how much content you can share - worldwide! You have a mission, a voice - and it needs to be heard! You need to get your word out to get buzz and attention.

I've helped celebrities like Tony

Robbins, Paula Abdul, Richard Dreyfuss, Darren Hardy, Jack Canfield and over 30,000 business owners, entrepreneurs, authors, experts, speakers, consultants and coaches promote, market and make more money online for nearly a decade in over 60 countries with our tools and systems and I know we can help you too.

The answer and solution you're looking for is right behind this button...go ahead, click it...

My guess is you want a lifestyle change, more control over what you do and how you do it... You want to get paid more for who you are, not what you do and are probably overwhelmed with all the tricky tools and tech, software, social media...maybe you're just getting started...

I know what that feels like. My passion is helping people get unstuck from tech and marketing quicksand to get seen, heard and noticed, make a difference and have more impact.

Go ahead - click the button and see how easy it is to get your message out to the world of billions of people and be seen on any device, anywhere, anytime?

Who wouldn't want that? I know I do!

What if I told you that there was a way for you to gain access to the multibillion dollar distribution networks the big brands control?

What if you could get your message in front of Apple's 500M customers who spend an average of $329 per year on their accounts?

How would you feel if you could get your message in the pockets of Apple's nearly 1.5 billion podcast subscribers?

If you look at the list below, you'll notice that you can get access to more than just Apple's massive customer base. The numbers for Google, YouTube, Facebook, and the other major social networks are staggering:

On iTunes alone, in 2008, 46.8 million Americans had listened to a podcast.

In 2012, that number increased to 75.4 million Americans.

In 2013, 125 Million (40% of US Population) - doubled in one year - and it's building even greater momentum worldwide.

Check out some of these other compelling stats below:

- There are 425M GMail users, 300M Google+, Over 1B YouTube users watching more than 4M views per day.

- Amazon has an estimated 220M accounts with credit cards on file, and they have more than 20M Amazon Prime members spending an average of $1,224 a year.

- Facebook has 1.23B active monthly user accounts.

- Yahoo - 281M accounts

- Twitter - 243M monthly active users

- LinkedIn - 277M

- Pinterest - 70M

- Vimeo - 100M monthly viewers

According to Pew Research, 73% of the human race is engaged with social media alone. When you add mobile phones to the mix, that total grows to more than 80% worldwide.

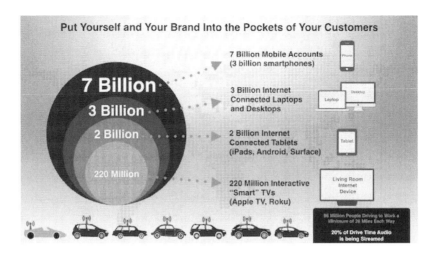

Put Yourself and Your Brand Into the Pockets of Your Customers

7 Billion

3 Billion

2 Billion

220 Million

7 Billion Mobile Accounts
(3 billion smartphones)

3 Billion Internet
Connected Laptops
and Desktops

2 Billion Internet
Connected Tablets
(iPads, Android, Surface)

220 Million Interactive
"Smart" TVs
(Apple TV, Roku)

Those big brands WANT you to create compelling, engaging, creative content and they will reward you by letting you connect, engage, and sell to their customers.

Why?

When you create excellent content, Apple sells more movies, music, and television shows. Google wants to sell ads around your content when people use Gmail, Google+, and YouTube. Amazon wants to sell more of your books and products so people will continue using their platform. When you post enticing, engaging content on Facebook, they sell more ads because their customer base stays on their site longer.

So how do you partner with them? What do these companies want?

New, interesting content. Without that, they are dead.

I'll prove it to you with a simple question: When's the last time you checked your MySpace account?

If your answer is "never", it's because MySpace lost the new, interesting contest battle to Facebook. MySpace has never been the same - the company never recovered.

Amazon, Google, Apple, iTunes and YouTube learned that lesson...and they are willing to hand over their PAYING customers to you in exchange for what they need the most... engaging content.

And they'll reward you by letting you seduce, captivate, and enchant their customers and users.

The first formula is simple - and because you're reading this book, you already have the three easy things you need to succeed:

- The first one is the **desire to help people**. You have to have a burning desire to improve someone else's life and well-being.

- The second is the ability to **answer questions** and share your opinion or to be able to ask another expert's intelligent questions. Your prospects have unanswered wants and needs, and you have to have the ability to deliver the answers to these questions. When you have a strong, passionate opinion (or interview an expert who does), your target prospects will side with you and rally around your cause and ideals.

- The third is you have to be able and willing to **give away and share your ideas**. The You, Everywhere, Now! system gives you the means to connect with nearly the entire human race *with the click of a button for free...*

If your initial reaction is "but what if I give away my best information, then they won't buy from me?" That's nonsense, and I'll explain why the reverse is actually true.

You have about 4-10 seconds to grab someone's attention, and you only have 1-3 minutes before they click to somewhere else. By giving away "your best stuff", you have an opportunity to get inside their minds, create a first impression, build rapport, make a friend, and get another chance to influence or persuade them to go the next step.

And once you begin to serve - they'll follow and hang onto your every word and come to you.

It's very simple for you create compelling content, and you might not realize it now, but you already have a complete production studio in your pocket.

A video shot with your smartphone looks as good or better than a $10,000 camera did from a decade or so ago; and with a simple, affordable microphone, you can record audio that rivals a professional studio from any smartphone, tablet or computer.

And in only 10 minutes, I will show you a simple strategy to build an active audience, get seen, heard, and distributed by the biggest brands and networks in the world. You'll be able to create compelling, engaging content that can educate, entertain, influence and persuade prospects to follow you, trust you, like you, and buy from you **_without being salesy_**.

Imagine what the access to almost the entire human race could do for you, your business, or the businesses of the people you consult with?

These are easily learnable skills, and with this book and our free resources, I'm going to show you exactly how to do it!

> If you want to see a side-by-side comparison to see a video shot with an iPhone compared to a $4,000 professional video camera with a $1,000 lens and more great strategies to share your message, products and services online, visit **www.TrafficGeyser.com/BookBonus** or text **YEN** to **58885** or text your email address to **(858) 866-8812**

Marketing Lessons from Buddha, Jesus Christ, Krishna, Mohammed, and Gandhi: How to Instantly Get Your Message on the Screens and in the Pockets of All of Your Target Prospects

> *"To me, we're marketing hope."*
>
> Joel Osteen

This chapter will reveal the psychology behind creating incredibly engaging, educational and entertaining content quickly, easily and cheaply that brings new traffic to your website or business.

You'll discover the system that CAN GIVE YOU an unfair advantage for leveraging the biggest brands in the world, grow your list, and capture the attention of more customers.

And it works around the clock, constantly building

momentum for you.

You'll learn a quick and easy distribution strategy that will get your message, story, and vision out to the connected planet. The bottom line is this will get YOU EVERYWHERE NOW with the click of a button.

And the best part? You can model the formula without spending ten years and tens of millions of dollars that we spent learning how to do it.

But before I do that, I want to answer some common questions and objections I hear from other entrepreneurs and business owners about using video and social media to grow their business or online platform:

- How do I get traffic?

- What if I'm not an expert?

- How can I build an audience and become relevant?How can I attract the news and media, celebrity clients, and customers?

- I'm not technical, and I've already got too much to do. How do I find people to do this for me?

- I'm afraid of being on camera because I don't like the way I look, sound, and I don't feel authentic. What should I do?

- How can I develop the confidence I need to create compelling content?

- I'm already overwhelmed, I don't want to learn one more thing that doesn't make me money now!

Do any of these sound like you?

If so, then I have good news for you - this book and the companion videos will save you time and erase these common challenges, concerns, and questions that took me years to overcome.

In order for you to succeed in this new age of marketing, YOU ONLY NEED TWO THINGS:

- GREAT CONTENT

- SEAMLESS DISTRIBUTION

In this book, you're going to see exactly how both are done.

When you create entertaining, engaging, and educational content, you'll be able to market your personal brand, your company, or your products and services to millions of people all over the world - for free!

You will be able to get on the screens, in the ears, or inside any pocket or device your target customers own, all while leveraging the world's biggest brands to grow your visibility and your list.

You'll learn how to partner with companies like Google, Amazon, Facebook, Twitter, Apple, YouTube, LinkedIn, and more– so you get seen, heard, and read all over the world.

The basic concept that gives you this power is something we call "Multicasting". It's the idea of being able to create your content once and then distributing it to virtually any device imaginable.

In the next chapter, I'll describe in detail what multicasting is and how it works, but with the power of Multicasting, right now you have the opportunity to have your own live or recorded television show and your own radio program. You could get published in virtually every newspaper, magazine, or blog imaginable.

This gives you the power to have instant distribution and visibility on any screen, pocket, or device anywhere at anytime. This gives you instant access to 73% of the human race (that's almost 6 billion people)

If you were taught how to do this, you'd be crazy not to do it, right?

Of course you would!

Here's the bottom line: you can do that right now when you understand and leverage multicasting. You can create content once and distribute it everywhere at anytime.

When you multicast entertaining and engaging content, you will harness the power of the "click economy" we live in today.

The businesses that get the most out of this will be the ones that understand this simple idea. When you finally realize the power of looking at the marketing of your business through this new lens, you'll understand why your business isn't different.

If I sat you down right now and asked, "What kind of business are you in?" Most people would say, "Well, I'm a chiropractor, or I'm a yoga instructor, or I'm a teacher or a financial planner."

Over the past decade, we've helped businesses in over 60 different countries improve their marketing. To illustrate how any business can leverage the power of Multicasting, here's a partial list of the types of businesses we've helped:

- Addictions

- Alternative medicine

- Animals / Pets

- Associations

- Astrology

- Automotive, transportation

- Caregiving

- Coaching & consulting

- Cooking

- Copywriting

- Debt management & money

- Dentistry

- Design / Art

- Education

- Entertainment / events / film

- Fashion

- Financial services

- Fitness, gym, weight loss

- Home business

- Hypnosis

- Info marketing

- Insurance

- IT / Support / Training

- Legal / Law

- Online marketing

- Management

- Music instruction

- Non-profits / charities

- Nutrition, healthcare

- Martial arts

- Parenting / Children

- Personal growth

- Photography

- Real estate

- Relationships / love / sex

- Retail

- Retirement

- Security

- Skin care

- Social media & local marketing

- Software

- Speaking

- Spirituality / Religion / Ministry

- Therapy / Counseling

- Trade

- Travel

- Writing / poetry / fiction

Whatever industry or niche you *think* you're in, you're likely thinking about it the wrong way because the reality is that you are in SHOW BUSINESS.

If you are asking yourself "why show business", let me explain:

Being in *show business* means that you need to SHOW your prospects and your customers that you care. You need to *show* them that your products and services provide hope to those who need or want to change or improve their lives. You need to *show* them and tell them inspirational stories that reveal how well your products and services work. You need to *show* them how to get motivated, how to take a risk, and how to invest in you and your business.

You need to *show* your target customers how to experience transformation. Once you do this, you're going to be providing results in advance, and this will change the future fortunes of your business forever.

When you think about it, Buddah, Jesus Christ, Krishna, Mohammed, Gandhi and every other spiritual leader taught with stories to connect with their followers, raise consciousness and deliver their message clearly and memorably. In a matter of speaking, *all of them were in SHOW business…*

Now before you fire off an angry email chastising me for comparing a great leader to a marketer - that is not a spiritual judgement. *This is nothing more than a marketing observation*, and I respect your spiritual or religious opinion whatever it might be.

Now don't get me wrong - providing results in advance and being in show business doesn't mean that you have to be a spiritual leader, professional actor, comedian, movie star, or look like George Clooney or Cameron Diaz (fill in the blanks with whomever you think is the most beautiful person in the world).

You simply have to teach and tell passionate, powerful, and engaging stories of how peoples' lives are changing with your message.

And when your audience is engaged with your stories of proof, hope, inspiration, motivation, and transformation, they will remember you. And when they remember you, they will think about you and they will refer you to other people.

If you've done all these things correctly, you'll start building a following.

Your momentum will grow, and your customers will transcend to higher levels of consciousness.

Your new following will trust you and get invested in you – and that's the big idea of 'You. Everywhere. Now!'.

And when your "tribe" are educated and entertained, they will buy from you, they will buy from you in higher quantities, and they will buy from your more frequently.

You're reaching every person and every device - anytime, anywhere. Your prospects and customers will be completely integrated so you can create your content once and distribute it everywhere.

Remember how I told you about the big brands that

control billions of eyeballs just waiting for you?

In this book, you'll learn how you can broadcast your messages live to audiences of millions of people at a time with free services like Google Hangouts or YouTube Live technology. After you broadcast your message, you can also distribute the audio free of charge on iTunes and then share your content on dozens of social networks.

Those networks control access to billions of people who don't know who you are, what you do, who you do it for, or why you do it - and its paramount that you show these people how your products, services, ideas or experience can help them.

The best part is, all of this can be done with the click of a button for free. In other words, Google could be sharing your message to billions of users and it will cost you absolutely nothing.

If that excites you, this book will reveal the right system, formula and tools to help you get, keep, and profit from your new flood of attention.

The Power of Multicasting:
Create Once,
Distribute Everywhere

> **"Marketing is a contest for people's attention."**
>
> Seth Godin

This is a graphical illustration of "Multicasting: Create Once, Distribute Everywhere to Every Device."

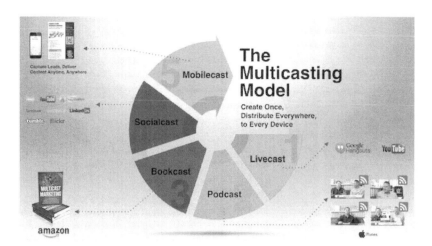

The whole idea is you can quickly and easily tap into yours or anyone's know-how, experience and wisdom, rapidly create engaging, compelling content, broadcast it live to any device, anytime, anywhere for free so that it can be viewed, heard and read on every screen, heard in any car, play in every living room...interactively.

Best of all, it's leveraging free, multibillion dollar networks. And if you know a few "secrets" about persuasion and influence, you can create compelling reasons for viewers, listeners and readers to interact with you from their devices.

Here are each of the five "casts" - broken down to show you what they are, how they work and how they make money.

We call these "Money Maps"

Money Map #1: LiveCasting

This is how to get traffic, leads and sales by leveraging Google Hangouts Online and the YouTube Live networks to give you access to over 2 billion registered users for free!

Right now Google reports it is capable of broadcasting to several million simultaneous viewers for free.

That means you can be watched and heard by as many as 1,000,000 or more users on Phones, Tablets, Desktop, Laptop computers or Smart TVs live!

It's a simple strategy that requires minimal equipment and can be used to rapidly create content, do live training and sales events. You can do them free or charge on a pay-per-view basis.

Because they're happening in real-time, you can have an interactive conversation with your viewers - whether there are 5, 500, 5000 or 500,000 viewers at once.

In our business, interactive Livecasting is responsible for 55% of our revenue and we consistently produce an average of $100-$400 per viewer who watch our live programs.

Personally, I think Livecasting is going to completely

decimate the broadcast and television market because it eliminates the infrastructure and broadcast expenses completely.

It's also a tremendous business opportunity because as more businesses learn about Livecasting and how affordable it is to interactively engage their prospects and customers, they'll want to find people to do it for them.

Providing Livecasting as a service can earn you $5,000, $15,000, $50,000 or more per day and startup costs and the training curve is minor!

Money Map #2: Podcasting

Podcasting is a great way to rapidly create content and get free traffic, leads and sales by partnering with Apple to start your own online radio or television show that can be viewed or listened to on any mobile phone, tablet, desktop or laptop computer or Internet enabled TV. Even cars!

Right now over 96 million Americans drive an average of one hour; 26 miles each way to work every day listening to audio and over 20% is STREAMING content.

Shouldn't they be listening to your podcast, your message, about your products and services for that hour?

Podcasts are delivered 100% of the time to subscribers. And, unlike email, the moment you press the "Publish" button, the podcast episode gets delivered within MINUTES to your subscribers.

How are you going to get all those subscribers who watch and listen to your shows? Once you create a your podcast, Apple will promote you to it's nearly 1.5 billion podcast subscribers, distribute your show and give you a free web site and a page in iTunes...for free!

Apple doesn't limit the number of shows you can create so, you could start a radio or TV network for free.

You can monetize podcasts a variety of ways including sponsors, advertising revenue, income from leads and direct sales.

When you read one of the next chapters, you'll see how Ed Rush started and launched a podcast and reached #25 on iTunes, got major sponsors and built a list of 25,000 in less than two months

The opportunity to create podcasts for clients and customers is HUGE and there's very little competition. Because so many devices are available that receive podcasts (billions), there is enough critical mass and momentum to support almost any business niche. Some of our members are charging $2,000-$5,000 or more per month to produce client podcasts for about a half a day of work!

Money Map #3: BOOKCASTING

It's easy to get traffic, leads and sales by partnering with Amazon and getting viewed and read on any mobile phone, tablet, desktop or laptop computer with "Bookcasting."

This book (and my previous four others) were created using the bookcasting model and we've taught THOUSANDS of people all over the world how to get published in 30-100 days.

Amazon has nearly 300 million paying customers and will give you a traffic-producing, search-engine optimized website free that will promote and market you and PAY YOU 70% commissions when they sell your books for you!

Some of our past customers including Sandi Masori created her book in under 30 days and got on the Today Show because she was a published author.

Another customer, John Cote wrote and published his book in under 100 days, got a speaking gig, closed a $12,000 deal creating a book for a doctor client with this formula

And a 9 year-old, Abbey Richter wrote 4 books in three months and is being featured on a cover of a magazine and being asked to speak and do book signings with her mom.

Books are an ideal way to generate qualified leads for any business.

Amazon lets you sell as many Kindle or paperback books as you want, will promote them, take orders, print, deliver them and pay you up to 70% royalties!

Creating Bookcasts for clients and customers as a consultant has very little competition. Some of our members are charging $4,000-$12,000-$20,000 or more per per book and have started six-figure businesses in a few months doing this for other people part-time and full-time!

Here's a snapshot for one month of royalties from just three countries for my Kindle books only - over $2,200 and this doesn't include paperback or a dozen other small countries!

Title	Author	Royalty (USD)
Sales report for the period 01-Feb-2014 to 28-Feb-2014		
Amazon Kindle US Store		
Instant Cus	Mike Koenigs	23.42
Author Exp	Mike Koenigs	1.05
Author Exp	Mike Koenigs	72.59
Life With Te	Mike Koenigs	0.35
Podcast Str	Paul Colligan	14.00
Podcast Str	Paul Colligan	125.00
Multicast M	Mike Koenigs	637.97
Multicast M	Mike Koenigs	1173.16
Total Royalty for sales on Amazon Kindle US Store (USD)		2047.54

Title	Author	Royalty (CAD)
Sales report for the period 01-Feb-2014 to 28-Feb-2014		
Amazon Kindle CA Store		
Instant Cus	Mike Koenigs	5.37
Author Exp	Mike Koenigs	10.20
Life With Te	Mike Koenigs	0.35
Podcast Str	Paul Colligan	0.76
Podcast Str	Paul Colligan	13.59
Multicast M	Mike Koenigs	20.52
Multicast M	Mike Koenigs	71.68
Total Royalty for sales on Amazon Kindle CA Store (CAD)		122.47

Title	Author	Royalty (GBP)
Sales report for the period 01-Feb-2014 to 28-Feb-2014		
Amazon Kindle UK Store		
Instant Cus	Mike Koenigs	1.12
Author Exp	Mike Koenigs	2.52
Podcast Str	Paul Colligan	0.26
Podcast Str	Paul Colligan	3.84
Multicast M	Mike Koenigs	31.06
Multicast M	Mike Koenigs	61.50
Total Royalty for sales on Amazon Kindle UK Store (GBP)		100.30

Money Map #4: Socialcasting

This is YOU. EVERYWHERE. NOW.

Once you've created your Livecasts, Podcasts and Bookcasts, you need to get the word out to the world by distributing your content to as many places as possible. We live in a "click economy" now and getting seen, heard and found is the key to success.

You can legally and legitimately borrow the viewers and customers from the world's biggest sites and brands including Apple, Google, YouTube, Amazon, Facebook, Twitter, LinkedIn, Yahoo, StumbleUpon, Reddit, Tumbler and many more that will actively promote, market, and share you with the world on every screen, in every pocket, desktop, laptop, smartphone, tablet, car and television.

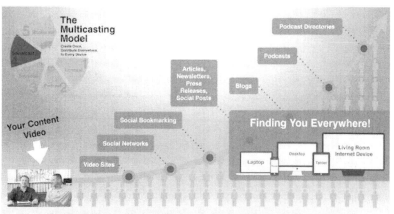

Socialcasting - Getting Found via Social Sites and Search Engines

These companies put you in front of billions of people so they can find and learn about you, your products and services anytime, anywhere on any device.

With a single upload, Traffic Geyser will distribute YOU to MULTIBILLION DOLLAR NETWORKS FOR FREE. You can schedule ten, hundreds or thousands of videos, images or social messages that can get distributed now, in days, weeks, months even years.

There's huge demand to do video, social media and mobile marketing for clients and customers. Many of our customers are charging $500, $2,500, $5,000 and more every month on retainer. Some of them have built 6 and 7 figure businesses just doing this.

Money Map #5: MobileCasting

This is where the money is made.

73% of the human race is using social media. Almost 80% have a mobile phone.

And more than half of all social media users are visiting web sites with their mobile phones or tablets.

And guess what?

Fewer than 10% of all web sites online today are mobile compatible. Most businesses are only capturing leads with one "channel" - most likely email on a lead capture form. And most of those lead capture pages aren't "mobile responsive" which means they don't work with phones or tablets.

If you are ONLY capturing leads with web pages and you're ONLY following up with email, then you're probably making about 30% of the money you could or should be.

Let's just say you SocialCast your videos, social content, images, your podcasts and livecasts.

Your goal should be to capture leads as many ways as possible and following up as many different ways as possible:

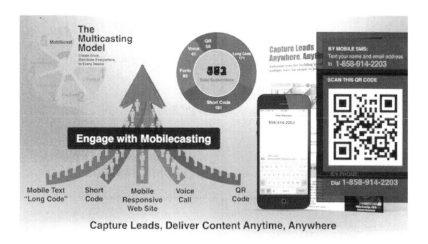

Capture Leads, Deliver Content Anytime, Anywhere

By Mobilecasting, you'll capture leads through multiple channels including:

- Mobile responsive web sites on Desktop and laptop computers, Smartphones and Tablets.

- Capture with mobile text messages

- Short codes

- Automated voice calls

- QR Codes

- And even business card scans

And you want to follow up with as many "channels" as possible too:

- With an email

- A mobile text message

- Voicemail message

- A video message

- An audio message

- Or even a podcast directly to their car or TV in their living room!

Do you see the power of this? Can you see how this is a total game-changer, a complete no-brainer?

This is You. Everywhere. Now. This IS the future of Marketing.

Multicasting Case Study

To give you an example of the power of multicasting, this is how I wrote the book, "You Everywhere Now" that originally began as a Podcast.

I used "Google Drive" (formerly Google Docs) to list some bullet points and notes I gathered during a brainstorming session.

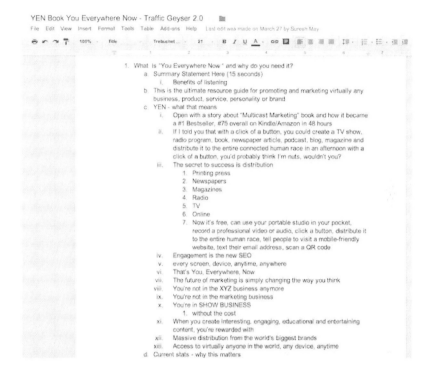

Next, I plugged in a $100 microphone into my Macintosh laptop and started recording the chapters as if I were teaching or being interviewed on a radio show. In real-time, I had my team Paul, Suresh, and Liz type notes for me in real time to keep excellent content and questions flowing my way. At the end of each "chapter" or episode, they asked me clarifying questions in case I missed or forgot something.

All of them accessed my notes and made tweaks, changes and comments while I performed each chapter… So even while I was talking, I could watch what they were entering!

Just to be clear, you don't need a team like I used to do any of this. It turns out I had a TOTAL of two days (about 16 hours) available to come up with the book content, dictate, direct and edit it due to an insanely busy schedule. I've found that I perform and teach better with an audience - except this is with an audience I pay for!

I could easily record the podcast as a video with my Smartphone or any camera. But for most people, it's easiest to start with audio.

The podcast recordings can be given away and distributed through Apple's iTunes service, and that's free of charge. Apple even puts my Podcast on their site (with a direct link to my site) and promotes the podcast on iTunes FOR FREE!

Apple has about a billion and a half podcasts that have been subscribed to. In the United States alone, there are approximately 96 million people who are driving to work every day, and they commute an average of 26 miles (or about 30 minutes) to work each way.

This means that these people can be listening to you and your message during their commute. When you talk about leverage in your business, it doesn't get more powerful than that!

After you create your podcast, anyone who sees your free content can subscribe to it through any smartphone, desktop or laptop computer, tablet or any Internet-enabled TVs. This will allow people to watch and listen to you anytime, anywhere.

About 20% of the people driving the 96 million American cars are currently listening to streaming content. And when you consider the worldwide reach in cars, we're talking about a couple hundred million people - and when you factor in China car sales, that number is growing at an incredibly fast pace.

After you create the podcast content, you can quickly turn it into a book and market it to Amazon and their millions of customers - just by having it transcribed.

I have my podcasts transcribed on various outsourcing web sites including Fiverr.com, edited by people I find on Craigslist, oDesk, Freelancer.com, eLance or Fiverr. In our training programs, we show you to find and manage outsource talent step-by-step.

I upload my books to Amazon Createspace - for free. This service makes the book available for download on any device in less than a day and will even make it available as a paperback right on Amazon and in bookstores all over the world...for free.

Anyone can buy your book with one click of a button. This gives you the power to have your target market reading your book on any mobile device, Kindle, or any laptop or desktop computer in an instant– and Amazon will even pay you 70% of the profits for the privilege.

You can also turn that content into an audiobook that can be sold through audible.com and a variety of other audio services.

The bottom line is EVERY one of these "channels" - livecasting, podcasting, bookcasting, socialcasting and mobilecasting results in being heard, seen and read on virtually any device. With the right incentive and offers, those listeners, viewers and readers are encouraged to get more information about you, your products and your services.

SocialCasting

After you've created your content and distributed it on Google, iTunes, and Amazon, the next step is to Socialcast the content. Every one of the episodes or segments of your podcast can be distributed and given away on the biggest social networks in the world.

You can put your content on all these services and they will link back and promote you. You can literally hijack (legally of course!) the biggest social media network brands and send their customers to your marketing funnels.

Hopefully you're seeing just how big this is, but it doesn't stop there - in a later chapter, I'll show you how I made over $1,000,000 in 43 minutes – and how you can make a boatload of money too.

Case Study: How to Go from 0 to 15,000 Viewers before Your First Podcast… Even If You're Not an Expert

My friend, Ed Rush, created his first podcast, "The World's Greatest Fishing Podcast". He really only started fishing seriously about a year ago. Now if you know anything about fishing, you know that most people don't become expert fishermen in a year!

Ed decided that he was going to create the World's Greatest Fishing Show after spending a couple days with a guide who he hired to teach him how to do halibut fishing. Ed was so impressed with the guide that he recorded a podcast with him and started a following on Facebook by posting pictures of himself and the fish he caught.

Before Ed released his first podcast episode, he had 15,000 viewers on Facebook by inviting members of other fishing groups on Facebook to his page, posting pictures and building rapport with his visitors. He signed up his guide to be his co-host. The initial fishing expert ended up introducing Ed to nearly two dozen other fishing guides.

Ed contacted all of them and scheduled eight 40-minute interviews with an initial group. And in just ONE DAY, he recorded eight podcast episodes.

That gave Ed enough content to not only have his own podcast and radio show, but he also started finding potential sponsors for his program - before he even released his first episode!

After only three months, Ed had 26,903 followers on Facebook and his podcast reached #24 OVERALL on iTunes! He's currently getting over 300 podcast downloads every day and that number is building momentum every week!

If you notice the screenshot below, it's not just 26 thousand plus likes on his page but more than 11 thousand are talking it. This nearly 50% engagement rank is almost unheard of on Facebook.

As of right now, advertisers pay podcasters about $60 for every 1,000 downloads a podcast receives each month and sponsors pay anywhere from $500-$5,000 per episode.

Most podcasters that support advertising have 3-5 advertisers for each 20-30 minute episode, so it's reasonable to make more than $10,000 per month or more with a weekly podcast that has only 10,000 downloads per month.

Here's the math and how podcasting can make you money:

10,000 downloads * $60 = $600 per episode per advertiser

If you have 3 advertisers, that's $1,800 per episode

And if you get one sponsor to pay you $700 per episode, that's $2,500 total.

Multiply that by four episodes per month and you're making $10,000 per month.

That's an extra $120,000 per year!

Inside our Traffic Geyser 2.0 training program, we include case studies and interviews from several podcasters including one who netted over $100,000 per month after just 15 months and is netting over $160,000 per month after only 18 months!

And we haven't even touched on other money-making ideas and ways to further monetize your podcast!

Ed is doing this to prove a few things:

- Anyone can start a podcast

- He's genuinely creating an income stream for himself because he's going to have sponsors and advertisers

- He's doing it all with a hobby that he absolutely loves, but he is not an expert.

- BONUS - Ed is also getting invited to go fishing with big name TV fishing personalities...and he was recently invited to be on a Fox TV fishing show. So podcasts can also open a TON of new doors for you too.

If you were on the fence about whether or not you could do this, now you know you can. If you're stuck, think about a few things:

- What's your area of expertise?

- If you're not an expert, what are you interested in?

- What's the message you want to share or show?

- How can you position yourself as an authority and expert?

- Who is your ideal customer?

Ed's story reveals that anyone can be in show business. If you're reading this right now, you can literally start an audio or a video podcast with nothing more than a mobile phone and a desire to get your message out to the world.

> If you want to watch and see more ideas and case studies about creating podcast shows and monetizing your knowledge, ideas, experience, wisdom and expertise with video, audio, books, social media and mobile marketing, visit **www.TrafficGeyser.com/BookBonus or text YEN to 58885 or text your email address to (858) 866-8812**

In the next chapter, I'm going to show you how to create

fans who will line up, wait, or even camp out for days in advance just to buy your products and services. This will blow your mind.

How to get Raving Fans and Loyal Customers like Apple

> *"If I wasn't an actor, I'd be a teacher, a history teacher.*
> *After all, teaching is very much like performing.*
> *A teacher is an actor, in a way.*
> *It takes a great deal to get, and hold, a class."*
>
> Richard Dreyfuss

In the last chapter I told you about a simple question I ask business owners when I first meet them: "What business are you in?"

People will usually reply with, "Well, I'm in the chiropractic business." Or they'll say, "I'm an author," "I'm an expert," "I'm a speaker," "I'm a barber," "I'm personal financial consultant," etc. You can fill in the blank with whatever business you can think of.

When I speak with many business owners about marketing, an interesting thing happens– just about everyone says "My Business is Different."

That's the #1 mistake most business owners make.

Marketing is marketing. In fact, like I said in the previous chapter, every business owner is in SHOW BUSINESS.

Whether you are in B2C or B2B, we're all in the business of getting more customers, staying relevant, increasing consumption, the frequency of a purchase, educating, entertaining, and adding value.

I'm going to share a story with you about the time I met the Academy Award-Winning actor Richard Dreyfuss, and how just nine days later, he was in my studio recording a podcast episode with me. This story illustrates the power of offering value FIRST and being in show business perfectly.

A few weeks before my team and I wrote this book, I was on my way to an event in Austin called "South by Southwest" - otherwise known as SXSW. On the plane, a guy in front of me said to someone he was traveling with, "Look over in the seat just across from you. That's Richard Dreyfuss sitting over there."

I looked over and sure enough, it was him. Growing up, a few of his movies really captivated me - Close Encounters of the Third Kind was one of my favorites. And "Mr. Holland's Opus" was one of the greatest movies I had ever seen.

I had tracked and watched Richard over the years and always appreciated his maverick style, willingness to be controversial and engaging and stand on his own when he didn't like something.

I texted my COO, Gene about the interesting "celebrity sighting" and he texted back 10 seconds later and said, "funny, I just listened to an interview with Richard about his foundation, "The Dreyfuss Initiative". Here's a link…"

THANK GOD for airline Internet!

I clicked the link and listened. I was blown away with what I heard… It was as though I had met a "brother from another mother"!

It turns out Richard started a non-profit called "The Dreyfuss Initiative". It's all about teaching civic responsibility and duty. But I didn't really understand the depth of his passion and desire to impact the country with his big ideas about civic responsibility, a return to justice and true democracy and cleaning up our filthy political system.

So, while I was flying, I learned a little bit more about what he had been up to.

Richard has been in 50 or more movies. He was also the youngest actor to win an Academy Award for Best Actor for "The Goodbye Girl" in 1978.

He's had an amazing career, but a while ago he just decided he didn't want to act anymore. He just quit and went to study at Oxford for four years.

And when he returned back to the states, he went to work and started his non-profit with the goal to teach and educate young people about getting back their voices and power and returning to the ideals of the founding fathers of the United States.

I really resonate with his vision and mission. I was inspired and I decided right there that I wanted to help him realize his goal.

And in an instant, I felt an idea hit me like a lightning bolt.

It turns out, I've raised nearly $2 million for my wife's non-profit "The Just Like My Child Foundation" and I really understand the challenges they experience.

I saw where I could add value to him.

Nonprofits need money.

I walked up to him on the way out of the plane and I said, "Richard, my name is Mike Koenigs and I love what you're doing with your foundation, The Dreyfuss Initiative, and I have some ideas about how you can raise money."

He turned around and he looked at me.

He smiled, pointed right at my face and he said, "Call me Rick. I need you."

We shook hands and strolled up the walkway, got to the end, and after we exchanged a few words I said, "So, where are you going next? I've got a connecting flight."

He replied, "I'm on my on way to Austin."

I said, "Well, I'm on my way to Austin, too. We're probably on the same flight. What's your seat number?"

He showed me his plane ticket and it turned out it was one seat away from me. I said, "Well, I'll talk to the flight attendant and see if we can sit next to each other." He said, "I think that's a great idea. Let's talk in the meantime."

We sat down and spent the next 20 minutes together. I learned everything about what his vision of the foundation was and the fact that he suffered back problems from a surgery and traveling was painful.

Richard is looking for other people to support the Initiative. I said, "You know what, I don't think you need to travel. If you had a podcast, your own online show, and you started learning how to livecast, I could show you how to broadcast on YouTube Live and raise $100 to $400 per person watching your program."

I said, "If you had a regular online show, developed a fan base, and leveraged your credibility and celebrity, you'd have yourself a hell of an opportunity to grab an entire audience to get behind you and start giving you money for your big vision."

I just shared with him the same ideas I shared with you.

I told him about Multicasting and the big idea about "You Everywhere Now".

I explained the whole idea of creating content once, getting distributed to multibillion dollar networks for free and legally and legitimately "borrowing" the viewers and customers from the world's biggest sites and brands including Apple, Google, YouTube, Amazon, Facebook, Twitter, LinkedIn, Yahoo and many more that will actively promote, market, and share your content with the world on every screen, in every pocket, desktop, laptop, smartphone, tablet, car and television. You can literally get in front of billions of people. They will be able to find and learn about you, your products and services anytime, anywhere on any device.

After that short description he turned to me and he said, "This is the coolest thing I've heard in years. It's revolutionary. How do we get started?"

And that's all it took to connect with a huge celebrity - offering value first.

He told me some great stories about his past, but mostly we just talked about where he wanted to go, what he wanted to do, and what his big vision is. We talked about impact. Making a difference. Legacy. Lots of big ideas.

Then I asked, "Have you written a book?" He replied, "Nah, I've been working on it. I've got about 200 pages done." I said, "Richard, you could have a book written in one month. I can show you how. I wrote three books while I was recovering from cancer treatment. If I can do it anyone can."

I explained Bookcasting to him. He replied, "Oh man! I need that, too."

By the time our flight landed, I turned to Rick and said, "I've got an idea for you. What are you doing next Friday?"

He said, "I don't know. My schedule is actually pretty open for a couple of weeks before I have another production."

I said, "Why don't you come to my studio in San Diego?"

"Bring along your key people who are involved in your foundation. I'll give you a strategy session about how to raise money and share your message and ideas with the connected planet. We'll just talk about what you should do and how you should do it. If you want to, I'll give you a tour of the studio, show you all the gear, and if I can support you, great; if not, you've got some ideas that you can use."

He goes, "That sounds awesome."

Nine days later, in walks Richard Dreyfuss into the studio and he's blown away. We sit down and we mastermind a big vision and I share the vision of "You Everywhere Now" to his team.

"Here's the big idea. You can put on a show and talk to one person, 100 people, 10,000, a million people at once for free. Google and YouTube will broadcast your message to the world. We can turn that into a podcast. You can give it away and you could put your message into the pockets, into the hands, in the ears, in the cars, and on the TV screens of billions of people worldwide, AND you can get promoted and marketed by Apple, Google, YouTube, Facebook, Twitter, LinkedIn and more."

We can transcribe the podcast and turn it into an Amazon book. He turned to me and says, "When do we start?"

I reply, "Well, how about RIGHT NOW? I'll have my team turn on the cameras in the studio at this very moment. Let's sit down and we'll make a show together. I'm going to show you how easy it is." He says, "That sounds great."

What happening next was pure magic: We sat down, turned on the cameras, and I turn to the camera and say, "Welcome to Digital Cafe, my name is Mike Koenigs and I have a really special guest here today, the Academy Award-Winning actor, Richard Dreyfuss, who is also the founder of The Dreyfuss Initiative. It's great to have you here, sir. Why don't you share with everyone watching this show what your foundation is and what your vision and goals are..."

We did an hour interview and he had the best time. I said, "Well, how do you think that went?" He goes, "I could do this every day." I said, "So do you want to do a weekly podcast with me? And he goes, "Yes."

The point is this: If you are willing to help people answer questions or feature someone else's expertise and have an opinion, or if you're willing to give away your ideas and your message then 'You. Everywhere. Now!' is for you.

It doesn't matter what business you're in, because no business is different.

You can be educating, entertaining and engaging. People

can find you because Google is out promoting and marketing you. Apple is promoting and marketing you. You've got Amazon that can promote and market you.

But what's so important here is it just starts by being able to tell some stories. Share your vision, goals and stories of hope, inspiration, motivation, transformation and transcendence.

When you tell your true, raw, uncut, authentic story, people will trust you, believe you, and magical things will happen in your business.

```
     To watch and see real-life transformation stories about
people who are successfully using multicasting to grow their
     businesses and making money as highly-paid marketing
consultants for other small business owners, entrepreneurs,
     authors, experts, speakers, consultants and coaches,
     visit www.TrafficGeyser.com/BookBonus or text YEN to 58885
           or text your email address to (858) 866-8812

     At the end of the first video, you'll see an entertaining
                music video, "My Business is Different"
```

In the next chapter, we're going to talk about the big opportunity and how you actually get in front of paying customers and how you monetize it.

How to Easily Partner with Big Brands and Seduce their Customers

The world famous copywriter Gary Halbert is famous for asking his seminar attendees "If you were given one huge unfair advantage, what would you need and what would you want?"

People would say all sorts of things like: "Give me a great location."

Or they would say, "Give me the best product, sales letter or celebrity endorsement."

After these people would finish, Gary would say, "I'll give all of you everything you want, and I'll still put you out of business with the one thing that matters most, A HUNGRY CROWD."

Gary is saying that one of the fastest ways to wealth is by getting your business in front of a crowd of people who want what you have to offer.

One of the best ways to get in front of a hungry crowd is by presenting your products to someone else's qualified buyers. If you could position a store that's right next to a complimentary store, you could make a lot of money very quickly.

You see this all the time: people have clothing boutiques right next to a yoga or workout studio. These workout studios have a lot of women going back and forth who are feeling good about themselves, and naturally they will just buy themselves a little gift as a reward.

I want to tell you a little story about how I "borrowed" a brand. When I started my company Traffic Geyser, everyone would walk up to me and say, "Mike, what kind of video camera should I buy?"

This is before mobile phones had really good built-in cameras, and you had only a couple of choices. Most video cameras cost $500 to a thousand dollars or so and they were pretty good, but they were still using tape. When some of the first digital cameras start coming out, they used chips or they had built-in memory.

Then Kodak came out with a camera called the Kodak Zi8 and it sold at the time for around 99 bucks. It shot really good 1080p high definition video, plus it had an external microphone input, which made it really great.

And every time people would ask me what camera should they buy, I'd show them this camera and I started demonstrating it.

After some time, I figured out a way to get that camera even cheaper, and this allowed me to give it away every time I sold one of my $2,000 training programs.

Here's how I did it: Because I love the Kodak camera, I decided to make a product demonstration video about why I love the Kodak and how it was better than the competing Flip camera.

I ended up meeting the guy who actually invented that product, and I walked up to him and said, "I know how to sell a whole bunch more of your cameras, and I also have a product or service that I think would compliment what you have."

Well, I showed him my little demo video and he went crazy for it. He started tweeting it and posting it online. This gave me an audience with Kodak, which led to me being able to buy the camera for about half price and use it as a premium to give away.

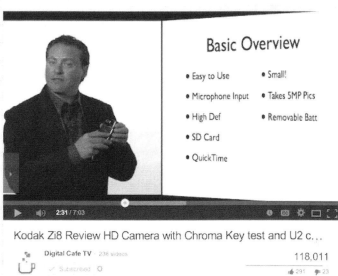

Kodak Zi8 Review HD Camera with Chroma Key test and U2 c...

I used Traffic Geyser to distribute that demonstration video online and the video quickly got over a hundred thousand views. I actually took the camera in a concert and I shot a little clip of U2 and the Black Eyed Peas as they were performing.

Afterwards, I named that video something along the lines of "Kodak camera with U2 and Black Eyed Peas footage." I borrowed someone else's brand and credibility three different times: I had U2, I had Black Eyed Peas, and I had a Kodak Zi8.

Well, that video got seen so many times that when you would search for Kodak Zi8 or Kodak Zi8 review, it showed up on the first page of Google. In my video description, I had a link in there that said, "If you'd like to win this camera other free video hardware and get product reviews, visit www.MikesGadgetGiveaway.com".

I would send people to my website who watched this video and they would join my list. I ended up building a list of over 8,000 names as a result of that. Kodak never did give me an opportunity to start promoting my product, but I borrowed their brand by creating a review.

So you may be asking yourself, "Where is the money in this?"

The answer is you use this idea of 'You. Everywhere. Now'; you use this idea of multicasting, of broadcasting your message all over the place, so you can get a following, get people clicking, watching, viewing you, and joining you in your social media networks.

BUT REMEMBER: just having a bunch of Facebook likes or just having a bunch of Twitter followers doesn't mean you're making money. Somehow you've got to get those people to follow you and join your list.

When you create product reviews, you can make them about books, services, or you can make them about other products. You can leverage their name by saying whatever the product name is in your review, and that's one of the most searched for keyword phrases that exists for that product.

You can literally put your personal brand in front of people who are already interested or who are already buyers of those other products.

Product reviews are one of the easy ways. Another really easy strategy is reviewing a best-selling book that's out right now. You could create a book review and post it online, make a live cast about it, and you can put it on YouTube.

This is what we call "Socialcasting", and you can do all of that with Traffic Geyser.

After you Socialcast your content, you can then do a Podcast episode about that product or that book.

To generate leads, you can say, "Look, if you buy this book on Amazon and forward your receipt to me, I'm going to give you a free study guide about this book, so you don't even have to read the whole thing."

The whole idea is a way for you to attach to someone else's brand, leverage people who bought that product, and get buyer names. If you approach any smart marketer and say, "Look, I'll give you a million names of random strangers and their email addresses or I'll give you a thousand email addresses of people who bought a product."

They would take the 1,000 buyers in a heartbeat.

If I had 10,000 email addresses for business owners who bought video cameras who want to make marketing videos, that would be incredibly valuable to me because I have software tools and training for people who want to do video marketing.

If you were a yoga instructor, it would be incredibly valuable for you to get a thousand email addresses of people who recently bought a yoga mat.

Think about how you can get in front of someone else's buyers who are qualified to buy your products and your services. Those are the kinds of shows and invaluable pieces of content that you want to be making.

If you're building videos and content around other products, you can build your brand and become famous. Then you can pick the big brands up as being sponsors for your product and your services, and this will allow you to create unlimited income as well.

When you're using our multicasting strategy and this 'You. Everywhere. Now!' idea, you can create your content live using YouTube Live or Google Hangouts, then you can chop it up and make podcast episodes, and you can transcribe them and turn it into Kindle episodes.

Socialcasting is the process of taking your content and making sure it's on every imaginable social network. So, if we make a video right now, we'd certainly want that video on YouTube, but we'd also want it on Dailymotion, Vimeo, and Facebook video.

Also, we'd want to make sure we put those links on Twitter, LinkedIn, Tumblr, as well as a variety of other places. The Traffic Geyser system does your socialcasting for you and it also does your podcasting for you.

Traffic Geyser offers massive power to help you get your word out there by leveraging all these other giant websites.

It really comes down to this: if nobody knows who you are, what you do, or who you do it for, then your business is dead.

It's important that you think of yourself as being in show business and that you create entertaining content where you're able to share and exchange your knowledge and your information. That would be my highest and biggest recommendation.

I'd also suggest borrowing credibility or borrowing a brand. You borrow brands by doing product reviews, talking about other people's products and services, doing book reviews, and who knows. If you do a killer book review, there's a high probability you can get a hold of that author and find out if you can interview them.

You can start creating content with someone else who's

already famous or more famous than you are. And believe it or not, the way famous people become famous is they start hanging out with famous people.

In the next chapter, I'm going to tell you exactly who I am and why you should listen to me. You're going to get an opportunity to find out exactly how I've come from nowhere, built my own brand, and how I've managed to create several multimillion dollar companies, and sell them.

I want to share these stories with you because I believe you can do it too.

To get more case studies on how you can partner with big brands to give you instant credibility,
visit **www.TrafficGeyser.com/BookBonus** or **text YEN** to **58885**
or text your email address to (858) 866-8812

How to Become a Celebrity in Your Market so that You can Persuade and Influence Sales

> *"Creativity is just connecting things. When you ask creative people how they did something, they feel a little guilty because they didn't really do it, they just saw something. It seemed obvious to them after a while."*
>
> Steve Jobs

My dad is a barber. I'm the oldest of four kids and I grew up in a small town called Eagle Lake, Minnesota. We were lower middle-class. And while I grew up, the town I lived in had a population of 763 - the sign didn't change for 15 years.

I remember driving by the stupid sign. I hated being in and from Eagle Lake, Minnesota. We didn't have any social status and there was never any "extra" money so I developed a scarcity mentality and started making money as soon as I could. If someone would ask me, "What do you want to be when you grew up?" I'd say, "I want to be a millionaire. I want to get the hell out of Eagle Lake. I want to be rich."

I don't know if you can relate to that at all. But I thought that if someday, I had a million dollars then life would change or be different. And it took me a long time to learn better about that old lesson that goes, "It doesn't matter how much you make. If making money and having money is what's important to you, you'll never have enough."

I am going to tell you the story about how I produced over nine million dollars in a single week - and it's all based on what I've shared with you in the book so far.

That might sound crazy to you, but it's also the story of how we grossed over three million dollars during a single "direct to camera livecast." That's basically a live infomercial where we sold a product online. I'm not telling you that to brag, I just wanted to share with you how sometimes what you think you want and what you really want are two different things.

While I grew up, I was horrible at school - I never learned how to learn and didn't discover until much later in live that I'm a "kinesthetic learner" - meaning, I have to "do" to learn. I can't sit still or focus when I'm sitting at a desk.

I'm the oldest of four kids. My younger brothers and sister got the attention, and I didn't feel important or relevant. I wasn't good at sports. I was kind of small. I didn't learn how to be disciplined and my dad was busy working all the time because to pay bills.

As a barber, you have to cut a lot of hair at five or six bucks a head to make enough to send your kids to Catholic school and pay for the house and everything else. We grew up eating out of the garden and catching a lot of fish. My dad was actually born on a tiny, tiny farm in North Central Iowa. He had one pair of shoes a year and he didn't get his first toothbrush until he was nine years old. His parents expected him to stay home and take care of the farm.

To say the least, we came from humble beginnings.

Here's what ended up happening that literally changed the course of my life: a neighbor loaned me an Apple II computer in 1981 during Christmas vacation while he was away with his family.

He knew we could never afford a computer, but he gave me the computer and I taught myself how to program over a weekend. My neighbor loaning me the computer and me teaching myself how to program turned into some great opportunities.

I became a consultant in a day.

My very first lead came from my dad. My dad was a talker, so he chatted up some guy in his barber chair. The guy said to my father, "We just got a new computer at our office." My dad said, "You know what? My son loves computers and he taught himself to program." "Oh really?" "Yeah." "Maybe he could come over and teach my secretary how to use that thing." My dad said, "Yeah, he would probably do that."

So I get a call from Roger Elmquist, the Prudential insurance agent. He said, "Why don't you come on over and teach my secretary how to use a computer?" And from there, I started my first consulting business. I was about 16 years old when I started getting my first clients, and from there, that built into one thing after another, and I became a serial entrepreneur.

Fast forward a few years later, and I ended up moving to San Diego to start a company. One of them became Traffic Geyser and over a period of about three years, we built the company up to making a couple hundred thousand dollars a year. I had two partners and a few employees by then, so nobody was getting rich, but we were making money.

Everything changed when we started doing something called "product launches". That's where you create a series of videos that show people how they can make money online, how to do video marketing, social media marketing, and mobile marketing.

So a couple years after we started the company, we did a

product launch that did really well - it was in December. I picked up my mobile phone to tell my parents about what had happened. My mom answered the phone.

I said, "Hey mom." She said, "Hi honey, what's going on?" I said, "You know how I've always wanted to make a million dollars?" She goes, "Yeah. I know. That's all you ever talked about when you were a kid."

I said, "Well, I just made a million dollars in a week."

"Well, actually a week and the twenty years it took to figure out how to do it. And the best thing is, I know how to do it again and again!"

She laughed and said, "Wow! That's great, honey! Your dad is outside. He's shoveling snow right now and the grandkids are coming over for dinner tonight. Do you want me to call him up and bring him in so you can share the news with him too?" And I said, "Yeah. Why don't you go and do that."

So I've waited and I heard her go to the door. She comes back and I hear my dad and he goes, "Yeah. What's going on Mike?" I told him the same story.

We all laughed. They were proud of me. But within 15 seconds, the subject matter switched to grandkids, the weather in Minnesota and what was going on in Eagle Lake Minnesota.

My parents were happy for me, but they couldn't care less about how much money I made. They're not motivated by it. I share this story with you to impress upon you that you could come from humble beginnings and do the same thing.

I learned a lot from the experience and about four months later on a Monday morning in April, we did it again. Except this time, I called my mom 43 minutes after we had opened up our shopping cart to share very different news with her.

She picked up the phone.

Mom: "Hi honey, what's going on? Are you ok?"

Me: "I'm great, mom! Mom, remember how I called you a few months ago and told you how I made a million dollars in a week?"

Mom: "Yes. I sure do!"

Me: "Well, I just made a million dollars in 43 minutes."

Mom: "Wow! That's a lot better than a week, isn't it?"

Me: "It sure is. I told you, I figured out the formula!"

Mom: "That's great. Your dad is outside playing with the grandkids right now, we're going to go out to the garden to pick some things to eat for lunch. Should I get him?"

Me: "Sure!"

While I was on the phone with my parents telling them about how I made $1 million in 43 minutes, a half an hour goes by. I can remember it was exactly one hour and fourteen minutes later, my CFO sent me a text message: "We just hit two million dollars in sales."

I interrupted my mom and dad while they were sharing what was going on with the grandkids, Minnesota, the garden and Eagle Lake to tell them about the two million dollars.

They were happy that I was happy. Until that week, they never really understood what I did or how I made a living except they knew it had something to do with computers and the Internet.

And from that point forward over the next six days or so, that product launch earned $9.1 million in gross sales and we did something that we call "Livecasting" today.

It's a live infomercial that's broadcast online. And back then, we didn't really know what we were doing, but we invited some of our customers who were making money and getting results from using our products on the show. These people were literally feeding their families with the tools and resources that we had given them, and they'd show up at our studio and we broadcast live to an audience who were watching our launch videos.

Our audience would be able to chat with us in real-time and ask questions. We'd talk to them and I'd say, "Hey, if you're just joining us right now, go ahead, introduce yourself, tell me your name, where you live, what you do for a living, and why you're here?"

I'd also ask, "What do you want to learn today? What do you want to hear about? What do you want that's different in your life that you don't have right now?"

We'd create these little engaging shows, but that one livecast produced $3.1 million in sales over a period of 12 hours.

And that's just a single launch. Over the course of about five years, we've done ten consecutive multimillion-dollar launches. What is important to know is that the strategies and the techniques that I've been sharing with you really work.

The strategies you're learning on how to rapidly create

content by thinking of yourself in show business is what's going to differentiate you, turn you into a celebrity, and build your credibility.

How King Arthur and the "Hero's Journey" Can Help You Connect and Sell

I'm going to give you our five-step formula for creating multi-million dollar launches. It all has to do with something that's called "The Heroes Journey."

Joseph Campbell wrote a book "The Hero with a Thousand Faces" in 1949 and he talked about how our brains are wired to want to hear transformational stories. My personal story is really the classic "small town boy done good." You can go back as far as you'd like to in time, and the "Hero Story" is a consistent hallmark in every spiritual, mythological story or parable.

Here is the formula and how you can use it in your own business, and it all begins with connecting with hope.

Right now you're reading this book because you hope you can learn how to promote and market yourself, how to build credibility, how to get paid for who you are, and what you know versus what you do. You're looking for a way to add an additional income stream to your business.

Maybe you've been doing the same thing for a long time, and you want to find a way to get paid more for who you are and what you do. Maybe you want to multiply your income stream, add an additional income stream, or you're looking for a way to have additional financial freedom.

You're struggling with something - you need to overcome a challenge to reach an end point or attain some kind of goal - money, power or something that one of those represent or mean to you. Everyone struggles.

So how do you get there? The answer is simple: create marketing content and turn your life into a movie that your ideal customer would like to listen to or watch. That's the secret.

So here's the basic formula, step-by-step. Basically, the five steps are hope, inspiration, motivation, transformation, and transcendence.

Let me explain what those are and relate it to you. So right now, you *hope* to get some results. You *hope* to get some sort of change in your life, but you're wondering how do I get there and how do I do that?

In order to effectively reach you, I share *inspirational* stories of transformation with you.

In our business, we do that by finding relatable customers and clients who have overcome common challenges in their life by using our products, services, books, training, events and certification programs to achieve their goals and dreams. We interview them using some formulas, we gather irrefutable proof of their success and achievements. Sometimes we interview their spouses, partners, customers or even children.

The results are incredible. They're emotional. Life-changing. And so good, you couldn't make them up. But when our new customers watch these stories, they relate to them. Their lives are changed just by watching the stories unfold. And they want the same thing they just experienced through someone else's *Hero Journey*.

You're in the business of inspiring your listeners, your followers, your watchers, and engaging with those stories. The stories form the basis for their *motivation* which leads to *transformation*.

My definition of transformation from a business and marketing perspective is to start by giving you HOPE that your life or business can change for the better or connect you to the dream that something you hope for is actually possible. That's followed by INSPIRING you with social proof that you can do it too. MOTIVATION happens as a result of presenting an offer to you that connects your vision of hope, exciting you to take action, and overcoming any objections you may have. This puts you in a pace where you're comfortable making a decision, all because I reversed the risk of investing your money in my solution or offer. Finally, when you implement and achieve your goals or result - the TRANSFORMATION actually takes place.

This was the important thing because if I've *motivated* you to say, "Look, I want that too," I could then motivate you by saying, "If you want that too, I've got great tools like Traffic Geyser and Instant Customer that will help you dominate your market. I also have tools that teach you how to write books and become the expert authority. I've got tools that teach you how to close deals and to sell more effectively. I've got tools that teach you how to turn your ideas into products you can sell so you don't have to trade your time for money."

After I give you the details on how to fulfill your hope, you would be motivated to take action.

Finally, there is *transcendence*. This occurs after the transformation takes place. It's when the customer or client is so happy with the results of what happened that they refer other people to you, your business, and your products and services. If it happens on a big enough scale, you "go viral" and word of mouth advertising and marketing drives sales to your business on a massive scale. This is the most important of all, and it's the hardest for most people to achieve because in order to achieve transcendence, your customers have to become your family. And when your customers become family and lead your community to promote and market for you, they'll do it freely and openly, and they'll asking nothing in return.

Look at Apple as an example. They are currently the most valuable brand in the world, and they have ravenous fans and followers. They call them fanboys and fangirls because these are people who live, breathe, and die Apple. They stand in line for days or weeks when the new iPhone or some sort of new hardware is going to come out. They eat up every single thing that Apple produces. Android may have some of that, but people are not standing outside the store waiting for a Samsung phone to come out because, frankly, it just lacks personality.

Apple is the most valuable brand in the world because they have shared and shown how you are more creative when you have that tool, and whether it's true or not, people always buy for emotional reasons and not for intellectual reasons.

So, again, we start with hope. I hope I can get my work done faster. I hope I can communicate with my mom more effectively. You're inspired by seeing someone with that new mobile phone or whatever it maybe. You've seen that they can make videos with their phones. They can record audios with their phones. Then you think to yourself, "I want that too!"

You're motivated to buy it and you might be motivated by an opportunity. It might be a sale or special or a bonus that you get, and your life is transformed too.

When I started, I got my phone and I started shooting videos with it. I put it on YouTube and suddenly 300 people liked my video, and I put it on Facebook, and that was a transformation. More people like me. More people follow me. I sold more stuff.

If all Apple did was grab stories of transformation and plaster it to their website with how lives have been changed with Apple gear and Apple equipment, they'd sell even more stuff.

If you did that for your business and all you did is share transformational stories of people who invested in your products, in your services, in you, if something changed in their life, you'd have more ravenous fans. That's transcendence. That's when you and your brand goes viral and people become ravenous fans. That is the process of what we call the "disruptasaurus philosophy" - literally disrupt an entire marketplace and moving them in YOUR direction with your content, your message and your ideas - by taking them on the "Hero's Journey".

It's our hero formula, and everything we do when we promote and market, we always begin with hope. How do you want your life to change? We inspire our followers with stories of transformation from people just like you who've experienced that.

We motivate you to invest in a program and a product because you can have that too. We have your back. If you don't like what we have, we give you your money back.

For those people who use our system and actually write a book, create a podcast, or publish content after using our system, I'll be your first customer. I buy your Kindle and physical book, I take a picture with it and I promote it on our social networks.

I do this because I want to support our customers, and it also shows proof that people are using our programs and getting results. When you do this for your customers, it's in your best interest because you're going to sell more books and it's going to raise and elevate your credibility and your success. It's a physical irrefutable proof that your strategies and products work!

We literally have hundreds of people who've done this already in all of our programs. We go out of our way to promote, market, and popularize them because that's how we create a transcendent tribe that goes out of their way to talk about us and share what we do with others.

Here we are on stage with a few customers who wrote and published bestselling books in 30-100 days using the strategies we teach.

Mike Koenigs

Here I am with a few bestselling books written by our clients and customers using our systems. They're getting and closing deals because they have powerful content that's working for them 24/7 - 365 days a year and adding multiple streams of income to their lives. This "social proof" is not only powerful, but their stories are the best marketing content you could ever dream for!

I make a point of buying a copy of every book from every one of our customers, taking a picture of it and posting on our social media accounts to drive traffic and sales to their livecasts, podcasts, books, events and products. It's more social proof our systems work - and if my network can help grow your business and help you get discovered, everyone wins!

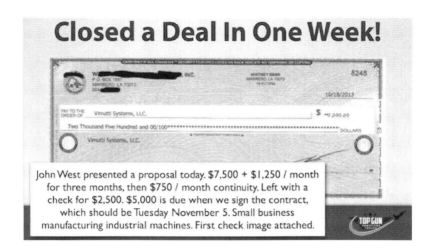

Closed a Deal In One Week!

John West presented a proposal today. $7,500 + $1,250 / month for three months, then $750 / month continuity. Left with a check for $2,500. $5,000 is due when we sign the contract, which should be Tuesday November 5. Small business manufacturing industrial machines. First check image attached.

Here's irrefutable proof - a down payment check from one of our clients who closed a deal in one week providing "Multicasting" services for a client. His first project!

So think about that. How can you use that philosophy in your own business?

The key thing that you need to do is ask yourself, "What transformation can happen inside my story for the viewer or the listener?" Remember, you're in the transformation business. If all you're doing is telling a story for puffery, that doesn't do any good. The reason I told the story about talking to my mom is because I wanted to expose the fact that I'm human. I'm a flawed human being and I made a ton of mistakes. At the same time, I want to let people know where I came from.

Most people can relate to the struggle that you went

through, and if you can tell a story that's relevant and resonates to your listener, then you can have a breakthrough in your business.

Mind you, resonance is a really important word here. That is how you build a following without being "salesy".

So if it's all about you and it's just, "Me, me, me, and me," there's nothing there. But if you have messages that relate with your customers by having them tell your stories for you, then you're on your way to building a powerful tribe.

If you don't have a story or you feel embarrassed, then that's twice the reason to share it because that will set you free. I guarantee someone would deeply resonate with that and they'll look at you from a different perspective.

In an upcoming chapter, I'm going to tell the story about how my wife built an incredibly successful foundation with a visit to Africa. Her story is very painful, and she has two major pains: She is the daughter of holocaust survivors, and this is one of the reasons why she decided to help stop a holocaust that was taking place in Africa.

The other thing is how she became an instant expert on nonprofits, on Africa, and on AIDS with a visit there, and how that is built into a foundation that raised million of dollars and transformed the lives of 600,000 people and saved their lives as well.

How to Build Your Online Power and Influence as Fast as Possible so that You Can Stand Out and Dominate Your Niche or Industry

> *"Don't let the opinions of the average man sway you.*
> *Dream, and he thinks you're crazy.*
> *Succeed, and he thinks you're lucky.*
> *Acquire wealth, and he thinks you're greedy.*
> *Pay no attention. He simply doesn't understand."*
>
> Robert G. Allen

In this chapter, you are about to discover the power of Multicasting and how you can create a number one best-selling book in under 30 days. I go into the topic deeper in my book Multicast Marketing: How to Podcast, Publish and Promote Your Content to the World with Google Hangouts, YouTube Live, Kindle Books, Mobile and Social Media, but this is a great overview of the process.

Paul Colligan and I had this notion a while ago and we

thought, "Okay. Well, we're coming out with a new product and a program, and we want to show this power of being able to multicast."

Multicasting is the combination of creating your content once with livecasting or podcasting and then distributing your content in multiple formats with bookcasting, socialcasting, and mobilecasting. You can put all these things together to build an audience, grow a list, and become an instant expert and authority.

Paul and I were brainstorming and we said, "Let's write a book and see how fast we can create, publish and promote a book to bestseller status." We finished "Multicast Marketing" in 17 days from concept to completion.

Here's what we did for this book - and our previous two bestsellers. Note that I describe this process as a collaborative effort although you can do it alone too. For me, I find its easier to have a "muse" to bounce ideas off of and check my ideas for the "nutty factor" before committing it to print :)

We collaborate online and brainstorm chapter concepts and some basic ideas for our content for the book and what we wanted to teach inside it. For the last book, we wanted to teach "Multicasting" and realized so much of what we were doing was educating people about how they could rapidly create content, become the instant expert and authority on any topic imaginable, and get their message and their content put on as many devices and screens as possible, and make money in the process.

It laid the foundation for what was eventually going to become "You Everywhere Now."

The brainstorming happens individually or together. We use Google Drive (formerly "Google Docs") as our primary collaborative tool. Paul lives in Portland and I'm in San Diego.

Over the next day or two, I keep the document open on my iPhone, iPad and laptop, constantly tweaking the outline, adding to it, editing and moving ideas around. I use Siri, Apple's voice-recognition software to make edits while I drive, go on walks or between meetings.

A day or two later, Paul and I get together virtually with Google Hangouts Online or Skype to interview each other. We talked about all of these different procedures and processes of what multicasting was and how to do it.

We record all these episodes over a period of a couple of hours, chapter by chapter, Q&A-style. I asked Paul a couple of questions, he'd ask a couple, we'd "riff" back and forth like two musicians jamming on stage. I would suggest an idea, "Hey, Paul. So let's talk about livecasting."

So right now, I could actually be talking to you with a livecast and showing you my screen. I could be demonstrating how my product and my service work. For example, if you ran a nonprofit, you can show people pictures and videos of what you're doing and whom it's helping. You could have someone join in from across the world with a video feed and you could interview them.

There's an endless variety of options and opportunities because that Livecast can be interactive and live in front of one person or no audience. If you want, you could just record it or it could be broadcasted live to tens of thousands or even hundreds of thousands of people.

Right now, Google says that YouTube Live is capable of being seen and viewed by hundreds of thousands of people simultaneously. I've heard rumors of it being able to be broadcast to millions, and all of this can be done for free.

Which, by the way, it a complete and total "broadcast killer" - in my opinion, this is the final "nail in the coffin" for broadcast, satellite and cable TV and radio. Anyone with a laptop and internet connection can broadcast live or recorded content to the connected planet, FREE.

When you post your event, Google promotes you and it shows up in Google's results, it shows up on Google Hangouts, it shows up on YouTube free. This is the "New SEO" (Search Engine Optimization) because the events get indexed almost instantly. You can buy cheap ads and clicks to promote it too.

As you can see, it's really a good deal - and all you need for your livecasting is a laptop. You could just do it with a webcam and a cheap camera or a cheap microphone, too.

Anyway, we ended up dividing the chapters of the book into podcast episodes. Those podcasts got edited and we put what we call front and back bumpers on there. It's the little animated logos and graphics. Then, at the same time we sent out all those episodes to be transcribed by transcriptionists, and then we pass that along to a book editor.

We put our book up on Amazon, Kindle, and in the first 24 hours we sold 90 copies of the book doing absolutely nothing.

Then, approximately over the next week, we ended up selling 2,038 books after that with almost no promotion. We really didn't pay that much attention to this, and all of that was done through Amazon.

Amazon gives us the great privilege of literally uploading your picture, your book cover, uploading your copy, which could be in Microsoft Word or a PDF file, and they convert it into a Kindle book. Amazon also converts your book into paperback, and they list it with Ingram, so your book is made available with the world's biggest book distributor.

So anyone at any bookstore can buy your book, and Amazon pays you 70% of the money while also giving you a free webpage.

After all of this is done, you've got one of the biggest brands in the world actively promoting you. Out of those initial 90 books that we sold, a big chunk of those came from people seeing us on Amazon and clicking to buy. We wrote that book some time ago, but to this day we're still in some of the top sales positions for this book and we've done nothing to promote it.

The book hit number one bestseller in advertising. It hit number 75 overall worldwide on Amazon Kindle bestseller. So we're among a ton of massive bestsellers. As a result of the sales of the book, Paul and I were listed on Amazon author rank as the number one and two most popular authors in business and investing.

Multicast Marketing: How to Podcast, Publish and Promote Your Content to the World with Google Hangouts, YouTube... by Mike Koenigs and Paul Colligan (Feb 6, 2014)
$0.99 Kindle Edition　　　　　　★★★★☆ ~ (6)
Auto-delivered wirelessly　　　#1 Best Seller in Advertising
Books: See all 8 items

THIS is what EVERY Author wants to experience -
A #1 Bestseller in a major category!

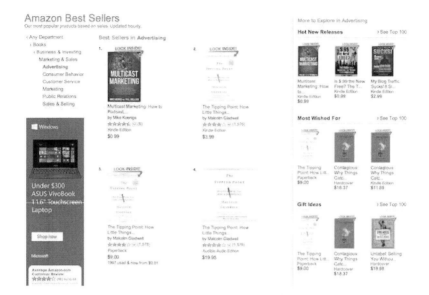

Look below - Paul Colligan and I were ahead of Malcolm Gladwell in Amazon Author Rank in the entire "Business and Investing" category and you can see in the image above that our book was outselling one of his best selling books, "The Tipping Point". We stayed on top for about a week - not long, but we didn't do any extensive marketing or advertising.

At this point, we had sold over 3,000 copies of our book.

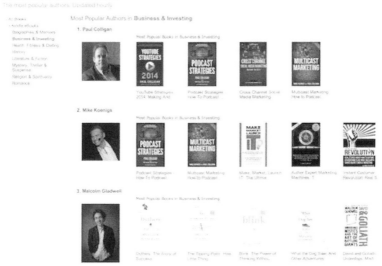

After we get all of this content, we go out and we can take all of it and Socialcast it. This means we can load up each of our episodes, pop it into Traffic Geyser, make sure it goes out to YouTube, Vimeo, Dailymotion, Facebook video, and all of the other video sites we support - and we're always adding more sites too.

It also gets social bookmarked on Facebook, LinkedIn, Twitter, Tumblr, and then we can use mobilecasting as our means of capturing leads.

But the simple answer is, if you have a product, a service, a message and an idea and you know who your target audience is, multicasting will work for you.

Here's what you have to remember: You are in show business. You need to be the expert and you need to be focusing on what you do and know the best.

So if you're good at doing certain things, then by all means do them. But if you can hire it out and leverage someone who can do those tasks, then focus on your core business.

You can use our tool Traffic Geyser to Socialcast and podcast for you. We also teach you how to do a livecasting in our course. We teach you how to do podcasting, bookcasting, socialcasting, mobilecasting, and how to use this practically in any business. We also teach you how to hire, use, and manage outsourced talent.

Those are the kinds of things that we will teach and educate you on when you invest in our programs and products.

A book is the best way to build your credibility, start a relationship, and get someone invested in you. If someone reads your book and raises their hand, they are essentially saying, "I want more."

And that's just the beginning: for some people, just reading the book isn't enough. They want that hands-on step-by-step training, someone to hold them by the hands, maybe even someone to do this with them. So what we want to do is we want to give you all of the tools and all the resources, and the book is the tip of the spear.

There's a step-by-step explanation of this process and how it works in **Free Video #1** and how to monetize this entire system in **Free Video #4** when you
visit www.TrafficGeyser.com/BookBonus or text YEN to 58885 or text your email address to (858) 866-8812

How to Make a Perfect Video Testimonial

> *"People will do things that they see other people are doing."*
>
> Robert Cialdini

Robert Cialdini is a social psychologist and author. His book, Influence: Science and Practice and Influence: The Psychology of Persuasion are the result of years of study into the reasons that people comply with requests in business and other settings.

Cialdini defines six "weapons of influence" - one of them is "social proof" (the others are consistency, reciprocity, authority, likability and scarcity but that's for another article).

That's what a testimonial is - it speaks to the viewer on an emotional level that they can relate to. Arguably, the most powerful marketing tool you can have in your arsenal is a testimonial. Lots of them.

Over the next few pages, I'm going to teach you the secrets to getting a "perfect" video testimonial. It's based on many years of experience getting BAD ones. I want to save you the endless frustration and wasted time of getting junk that doesn't help you and your business.

And I'll cut right to the chase: most people don't understand what a good testimonial is and if you just turn on a camera and ask them to say nice things about you or your business, you're not going to get what you need to really sell your products or services.

There's a system, structure and "nuance" to creating outstanding testimonials - and I'm going to share with you exactly what that is.

So if you can give your customer or client a basic structure to use and have them tell THEIR story about you, your product or your service, you'll get what you need every time.

And best of all - the more testimonials you get, the more you'll sell which will give you even more great testimonials!

Let's begin with what I consider to be several excellent testimonials...

BTW, I highly recommend you pick up a copy of "Influence" - it's cheap, and it's (currently) only $12.23

on Amazon:

——Testimonial #1——

"38 Year Old Mother of Triplets makes $25,770.23 in April and $18,036.74 in May with Traffic Geyser"

"I leave in Saint Charles, Missouri which is a suburb of Saint Louis, Missouri. I'm 38 - years-old.

I am a mother of 2-year-old triplets and they are all girls. I'm also a wife. I started a business in February 2008. It's all about marketing, helping a few service providers and elder care providers market their businesses.

In October of last year, I found Traffic Geyser and we added a new service which was video upload and some SEO and social media marketing to our suite of services.

In March we did $15,000 on a product launch in one hour. Part of our secret sauce is the use of Traffic Geyser.

I wanted to tell you all of this because I work from home, I am a mom, a wife, have employees, and everyone depends on riding this "train." It's a big thing to have a lot of people depending on you. With Traffic Geyser added to our suite of services, we have been able to afford a very comfortable lifestyle.

As of May, we are generating over $18,000 in revenues per month.

I haven't seen June revenues yet but we are expecting the same, if not more. We were doing ok before we implemented Traffic Geyser but now we're really doing an outstanding job. As long as you're around, we're around. Thanks Traffic Geyser!

Valerie VanBooven, RN

——Testimonial #2——

"Laid-off Construction Worker Dominates Google Page One and Increases Video Views by 740% in LESS THAN 48 HOURS, Starts Two Successful Online Businesses and Makes $11,800.00 From a Single Contract With No Internet Marketing or Video Experience"

"Patrick Mattingley here from Denver, Colorado. I want to tell you how Traffic Geyser literally turned my life around.

I know it sounds dramatic, but it's the truth.

You see, after years in construction sales, I was laid off in 2008 due to the economic downturn. I had no job, no income, and it seemed only a matter of time before the Repo Man would be knocking on my door.

But then a buddy told me about Traffic Geyser. Back then I didn't even know what online video meant, but I decided to give it a try.

In less than 48 hours, my video was dominating page ONE of Google results.

Yes, my video had 9 out of 10 listings on the FIRST page of Google results! Most people wait months, even years, for results that amazing, but with Traffic Geyser, it took LESS THAN TWO DAYS!

My video views went from around 15 to 112 in a matter of hours. I'm no math guy, but that's something like a 740% increase! That's an ENORMOUS jump, and in SUCH a short time.

Honestly, getting spectacular results that fast really blew my mind.

For the first time in months, my future looked bright. Little did I know, that was just the beginning!

My video got so many views, I started a video marketing business. Then, hoping to return to my career "roots," I put together a separate website for my new construction company.

Now, thanks to Traffic Geyser, I get HUNDREDS of hits on my new construction company site every month, which means as many as four leads on a single day, ALL of which can result in BIG-dollar profits!

Plus, my video marketing business continues to grow. In fact, I just got a signed contract from a client for $11,800.00!

So now I've got TWO successful online businesses, and just like that, my future is looking better than ever!

All thanks to Traffic Geyser.

If you're not using Traffic Geyser for your online business, well, don't blame me if the Repo Man shows up at your front door. It's so easy to use, and you get TONS of great support. Honestly, if I can get these kinds of great results, you can too.

-Patrick Mattingly

——Testimonial #3——

"I'm getting at least 3 calls a day worth an additional $20,000 to $25,000 per month"

"My name is Larry Stevens, from Clear Lake, Iowa.

I sell granite countertops in several local communities.

Ever since the economy took a downturn, our marketing costs have doubled and the number of leads we get every month has decreased by half.

117

I'm not a web expert or technical person.

Last fall, I wasted $58,500 on traffic generating systems that don't work. I blew $4,644 on Google AdWords and didn't get a single sale.

Three months ago, I discovered Traffic Geyser. I followed the easy training videos, made my first videos and pushed a few buttons. In just a few days, my videos dominate Google's top 10 listings - that I don't pay a dime for!

Best of all, I get at least three phone calls a day from new customers off these videos--which translates into $20,000 to $25,000 additional sales a month.

Before I used online video I got 3 calls a month and worked 60+ hours per week using marketing that didn't work.

Thanks Traffic Geyser - you've helped me more than double my business so I can spend more time with my family and pick up my kids from school every day.

My wife thanks you too because we're taking our first vacation in 3 years! She's happy because she has her husband back!"

———

Now that's a testimonial!

Full disclosure: the last testimonial is based on a real testimonial from a real customer but I used some of the techniques below to humanize it more and make it more powerful. The others are unedited, directly from the customer.

Tips and Strategies to Get Even Better Testimonials

Often times the "why" we do things has far greater value than the "how" we do things. For if we understand the why, the how typically takes care of itself.

The ideal testimonial should be NO LONGER than 60 seconds. That's plenty of time to tell a story, get to know someone and establish "likeability" and credibility.

In a 30-second testimonial, the "why" we give a testimonial can be divided into three segments measuring 10 seconds each in delivery. It is critical they are delivered concisely and in the following order:

1. Humanizing (10 seconds). This makes you a real live person with whom people can identify and relate. This is especially poignant for stay-at-home moms!

- Name (first and last)

- Where you live (city and state)

- Professional background (what you do, or did, for a living.

Expose a personal weakness or loss:

- "I'm a technical dunce"

- "I don't know anything about marketing"

- "I've wasted over $55,000 on traffic generating systems that don't work"

- "I blew $6,500 on Google AdWords and didn't get a single sale"

- "Ever since the economy took a downturn, our marketing costs have doubled and the number of leads we get decreased by half"

- "I've spent over $35,000 on web sites that don't work because the designers and technical people don't understand my business"

2. Product Testimonial (10 seconds)—This sets the stage for your business testimonial. Without your product testimonial, your business testimonial is incomprehensible. We must assume our target audience doesn't know anything about our opportunity. Your product testimonial becomes the logical "how" segue to your business testimonial.

- How long have you been using Traffic Geyser?

- How long did it take to learn how to use it and broadcast your first content?(for most people, it only takes about 15-20 minutes so talk about how easy it was to learn how to use it and if you're non-technical, state that too)

- Explain the personal benefits you got as a result of using Traffic Geyser such as:

    How much more money did you earn? (be precise)

    How many hours per week did you save?

    How many more sales are you getting?

    How many more phone calls or leads are you generating?

    How many more speaking opportunities are you receiving?

    Exactly how much money on marketing costs are you saving?

    How many Google Top 10 positions do you have for your keywords?

    What things are you able to do yourself that

used to require technical people?

3. Income or Benefit Testimonial (10-20 seconds)—Now that you've given your product testimonial, you can logically establish the reason for your monetary or benefit success. NOTE: Don't think you have to be making thousands of dollars per month to count. The mean income in the U.S. is roughly $27,000 per year.

Mary Kay has the perfect formula. If you can answer these questions, you've got a winning product...

- "Is it Easy?"

- "Does it work?"

- "Can I do it?"

- or "Will it work for me?" or Will it work in my business?"

- So if your testimonial answers those three things, it's perfect. You want the viewer, listener or reader to say, "hey, I can do that too!"

- Use a transitional statement (ex. "Because of my great results with Traffic Geyser, I'm not only making more money and generating more leads, but I'm saving 3 hours a week that I used to spend marketing and able to pick up my kids from school every day...I even joined a gym and lost 10 pounds!")

- Stay away from how you did it, jargon and technical mumbo-jumbo. The viewer will only remember the size of your check, the massive cost savings, major benefits or the growth of your organization.

- Turn the message back to the product or service you're doing the testimonial for (ex. "Thanks Traffic Geyser, your system changed my life!")

Tips and Requirements for Great Testimonials

- You don't need fancy equipment. A smartphone or Skype Video is fine.

- Be real. Don't act. Speak to the camera like it's your best friend, your son, daughter, wife, mom or dad. The moment you turn your testimonial into a commercial, it loses it's value and credibility immediately. Don't try to sell anything. Just tell your story and use examples.

- Precise numbers are more believable than giant round ones. "Increased my sales $38,481.69 between July 5th to the 23rd" is much more powerful and believable than "made $50,000 in one month" or "increased my income $500,000 the first year."

- Pause. Take your time. Don't worry about being perfect. Nobody is expecting you to be a movie star. REAL people make mistakes. Actors don't. Real people don't believe actors. We live in a cynical society.

- If you have any props, screen captures, checks, invoices or can show proof of the results you have achieved with the product or service, it adds massive believability and trust to the testimonial.

- NEVER READ A TESTIMONIAL FROM A SCRIPT. It's ok if you have a few notes in front of you that you refer to but do not use a teleprompter, cue cards or read a script. This will guarantee your testimonial is worthless.

- KEEP IT SHORT. Anything longer than a couple minutes is too long unless there's tons of proof or you're really entertaining.

- Don't advertise your business. There can only be one hero in a testimonial (that's the company or person you're doing the testimonial for, not you) - your goal and outcome is to tell your story in a compelling way that has emotional impact. The person or company you're doing the testimonial for WILL MAKE YOU A SUPERSTAR - YOU DON'T NEED TO TALK ABOUT YOURSELF.

- Don't shoot your video with a light or window behind you. Face the light or all the viewer will see is a silhouette.

- Shoot your video in a quiet room, free of pets, kids, phones and traffic.

Lastly, there is a clear difference between a testimonial and an endorsement.

A testimonial is your own personal experience.

For instance, "I started using Traffic Geyser and got a Google Top 10 in 24 hours and 3 new leads the first week that generated over $16,484" is a testimonial.

By contrast, "This is the best opportunity in the world and everybody on this call should join Traffic Geyser," is an endorsement. An endorsement is your opinion and not relevant to your testimonial. Just stick to testimonial material and you'll be fine.

Tip: Once you've recorded a few testimonials, you can broadcast them out with Traffic Geyser! They'll work like crazy to get you visibility, rankings and traffic!

Let's Create a Perfect Testimonial Right Now!

If you've watched a few Traffic Geyser training videos

and submitted them with Traffic Geyser, you're getting ranking, traffic and leads.

Note: IT DOESN'T HAVE TO BE PERFECT. IF YOU DON'T HAVE ALL THE PIECES OR PARTS, THAT'S OK! JUST RECORD SOMETHING!

The Perfect Testimonial Template

"My name is _____, I'm from from _____, _____. [name] [city] [state]

I _____ for _____. [profession/what you do] [who you do it for]

_____

[Expose a personal weakness, challenge, pain or loss - for example:

"Ever since / I'm not good at / I'm experiencing / major pain or challenge."]

_____

[Describe how things have been: losing money, wasting time, never seeing my kids, working too much, affecting my health]

_____

[Describe your major discovery - and what happened:

e.g. "I signed up for Traffic Geyser and got my first video online in a day. I built my first web site with the lead capture system in ten minutes"]

[Describe how things are now, how much more money you're making, more traffic, visitors and leads - BE SPECIFIC]

[Show proof with a prop if possible - be very specific, pictures, screen captures, check, printed page with an email: e.g. "here's proof, a copy of a check for $11,323", "I'm ranked in positions 3,4,5,8 on page 1 of Google", "I get an average of 3 additional leads per week that bring in at least $7,000 more per month", "here's the new BMW 330 Convertible I just bought this month"]

[How will Traffic Geyser change your income, business, free time, your health, your family or your ability to contribute to a higher cause? "I increased my revenue by 20% in 30 days, decreased my marketing expenses by 15%, doubled my sales, am working an average of 4 fewer hours per week and spending more time with my family"]

[Bonus: what does your spouse/kids/friends/co-workers/peers say?

"My kids are so happy they get to see their dad more and my entrepreneurial friends want to know what my secret is"]

[Closing: "Thank you Traffic Geyser for BIG BENEFIT "Thanks Traffic Geyser for helping me make more money and giving me the confidence that I can be a marketer too. I never thought I could do it myself because I don't know a thing about technology, video or online marketing but I'm living proof that if I can do it, you can do it too."]

> To see examples of high-quality video testimonials, social proof and really happy customers who have received excellent results, watch Video #3 in our free video training series.
>
> To get all the videos and updates to this book:
> visit www.TrafficGeyser.com/BookBonus or text YEN to 58885
> or text your email address to (858) 866-8812

How to Capture a Perfect Testimonial with an Interview

I've told clients for almost 20 years that if they only did one thing to promote and market their business, that they should capture audio and video testimonials and post them on their website along with a buy button.

The best way to build a library of testimonials is to capture them when the customer is present - at your office, studio, store, live event or a chance meeting.

Before doing the interview, let them know what questions you'll be asking them and have them bring some kind of physical proof they can show of the benefits they've achieved if possible.

Make sure you ask them to be SPECIFIC with their replies. Don't be afraid to ask them to try again.

- What's your name, where do you live, what do you do for a living?

- What was life like before Traffic Geyser? What challenges have you been experiencing in your business?

- When did you sign up for Traffic Geyser?

- What results have you achieved with Traffic Geyser (specific time, money, traffic, leads)?

- How long did it take to get results?

- What is life going to be like in the future now that you're using Traffic Geyser?

- What do your friends, family, co-workers or partners say?

Coach them to keep each response short and to the point.

That's it!

Here's how I get "remote" testimonials from customers. I send them this information along with the copy below in an email. (and BTW, if you're an existing customer, feel free to send your testimonial over so we can feature you in an upcoming launch, presentation or on your web site - it's fantastic visibility for you and your business!)

Now you can do it yourself - just:

- Fill in the form above

- Think about what you want to say

- Push the button on your camera

- Turn the camera around and start talking

When you're done, either email the video or a link to info@TrafficGeyser.com.

You'll also want to upload the video to YouTube or broadcast it with Traffic Geyser. Please use "Traffic Geyser" in your tags and add "Traffic Geyser Testimonial YOUR NAME - BIG BENEFIT" in the title.

Then send a link to your YouTube video to Support@TrafficGeyser.com.

It doesn't have to be perfect! Just do it and we'll make you famous!

Thanks!

Mike

PS - make sure you request that everyone fills out a testimonial/release form. A sample form follows this page.

PHOTO/TESTIMONIAL RELEASE FORM

PERMISSION TO USE IMAGE/TESTIMONIAL DATA

I, _____, give
_____ (herein, "
Company"), its employees, designees, agents, independent contractors, legal representatives, successors and assigns, and all persons or departments for whom or through whom it is acting, the absolute right and unrestricted permission to take, use my name, testimonial and biographical data and/or publish, reproduce, edit, exhibit, project, display and/or copyright photographic images or pictures of me or my child(ren), whether still, single, multiple, or moving, or in which I (they) may be included in whole or in part, in color or otherwise, through any form of media (print, digital, electronic, broadcast or otherwise) at any campus or elsewhere, for art, advertising, recruitment, marketing, fund raising, publicity, archival or any other lawful purpose.

I waive any right that I may have to inspect and approve the finished product that may be used or to which it may be applied now and/or in the future, whether that use is known to me or my child(ren) or unknown, and I waive any right to royalties or other compensation arising from or related to the use of the image or product.

I release and agree to hold harmless Company, its Board of Regents, officers, employees, faculty, agents, nominees, departments, and/or others for whom or by whom Company is acting, of and from any liability by virtue of taking of the pictures or using the testimonial/biographical data, in any processing tending towards the completion of the finished product, and/or any use whatsoever of such pictures or products, whether intentional or otherwise.

I certify that I am at least 18 years of age (or if under 18 years of age, that I am joined herein by my parent or legal guardian) and that this release is signed voluntarily, under no duress, and without expectation of compensation in any form now or in the future.

_____ Name (Please print)

_____ Signature

_____ Date

Signature of legal guardian if under 18 years of age:

_____

To learn more about how how you can use video testimonials
and transformational stories for your business and in your
marketing, join us for one of our **Free Monthly Livecast
Events** where you'll see step-by-step demonstrations and
examples of how to use the strategies in this chapter and
book to get more traffic, leads and sales for your business

**visit www.TrafficGeyser.com/BookBonus or text YEN to 58885
or text your email address to (858) 866-8812**

What's Next?

"Inaction breeds doubt and fear. Action breeds confidence and courage. If you want to conquer fear, do not sit home and think about it. Go out and get busy."

Dale Carnegie

At this point you are asking yourself, "What do I do with this?"

Easy. Just Do It.

Like anything in life that matters, it requires a little preparation and implementation.

The great news is we've created a complete step-by-step system that combines easy tools and all the training you need in one place to enhance and grow your own business or create multiple streams of income as a highly-paid consultant or coach to other businesses either part-time or full-time.

We've been helping businesses and people achieve their dreams for nearly a decade from virtually every walk of life and country in the world by getting noticed, getting found, learning the most valued skills in the world.

We can help you to - and the training you need to learn more and get started is free. Every product and course we sell includes a 30-day, no questions asked money back guarantee.

We have thousands of successful customers from all over the world who have made money and impacted lives as a result of believing in themselves and taking the first step.

Will you?

```
Complete details of the system are available in Video #4:
visit www.TrafficGeyser.com/BookBonus or text YEN to 58885
         or text your email address to (858) 866-8812
```

About Traffic Geyser

What if, with the click of a button, your message could reach billions of people and be seen on any device, anywhere, anytime? In the past, this has been a nightmare to make this work - complicated, time-wasting and really expensive.

Since 2007, Traffic Geyser has been the #1 tool for "socialcasting" - distributing videos and social media content all over the web with the click of a button to the best video, social media and networking sites including Google, Apple, YouTube, Amazon, Facebook, Twitter, LinkedIn and many more to billions of smartphones, tablets, laptop and desktop computers...even cars and televisions. There's no limit to how much content you can share - worldwide! You have a mission, a voice - and it needs to be heard! You need to get your word out to get buzz and attention.

Simply upload your video, picture, audio or text, choose the places you want your content to be distributed, "tag" it, press the submit button and your content is "Multicast" to dozens of places, all over the web so you can be found, build buzz, grow an audience and get more traffic, leads and sales for your business.

Since it's release, Traffic Geyser has distributed millions of videos for tens of thousands of customers in over 60 countries in virtually every imaginable niche and industry.

Traffic Geyser gives you the ability to distribute thousands of videos and social content every month for your business or for your clients. Traffic Geyser 2.0 is integrated with Instant Customer.

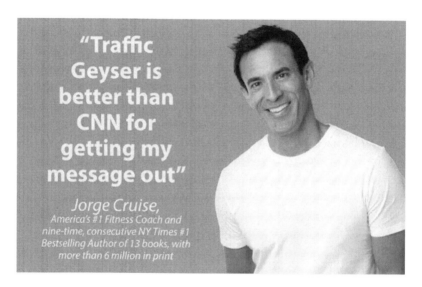

"Traffic Geyser is better than CNN for getting my message out"

Jorge Cruise,
America's #1 Fitness Coach and nine-time, consecutive NY Times #1 Bestselling Author of 13 books, with more than 6 million in print

About Instant Customer: Automate Your Sales and Marketing

Most business owners know they can do a much better job capturing leads, following up and automating their marketing. How about you?

Celebrity customers including Jack Canfield, Brendon Burchard, Darren Hardy (publisher of Success Magazine), Peter Diamandis (XPrize Founder), #1 Bestselling Author Daniel Amen, Richard Dreyfuss, Joe Polish and many more all use Instant Customer to grow and automate their businesses.

What if you could be in the POCKETS of billions of potential prospects or customers 24/7? That's MOBILECASTING - the unique cross-channel marketing capability only Instant Customer has is all about -

delivering your message and content anytime, anywhere and to any device!

Instant Customer is the only fully-integrated marketing and CRM system that captures leads with email, mobile, voice, QR codes and mobile responsive web sites and follows up with email, mobile, voicemail and integrates with over 250 systems including InfusionSoft, SalesForce, AWeber, MailChimp, SendOutCards, Kajabi and more. Instant Customer includes "Marketing Machines" for capturing leads from the stage, building membership sites, managing podcasts, selling books and much more.

To try Instant Customer today, visit www.InstantCustomer.com and get thousands of dollars worth of free video and social media marketing training. Instant Customer subscribers get FREE BUSINESS CARD SCANS so head on over to the iTunes or Google Play store right now to download the Instant Customer app!

Made in the USA
San Bernardino, CA
18 April 2014